Your Better Self
Study Manual

YOUR BETTER SELF STUDY MANUAL

A Simple Guide for Living on Purpose in Peace and Prosperity

Ken Wallace

authorHOUSE®

AuthorHouse™
1663 Liberty Drive
Bloomington, IN 47403
www.authorhouse.com
Phone: 1-800-839-8640

First published by AuthorHouse   09/26/2011

ISBN: 978-1-4520-7904-2 (sc)
ISBN: 978-1-4520-7905-9 (ebk)

Library of Congress Control Number: 2011907995

Printed in the United States of America

Any people depicted in stock imagery provided by Thinkstock are models, and such images are being used for illustrative purposes only.
Certain stock imagery © Thinkstock.

This book is printed on acid-free paper.

ABOUT THE AUTHOR

Ken Wallace is a professional speaker, consultant and executive coach specializing in personal and organizational development. He helps people and organizations do better than their best at anything they undertake.

For the past twenty-one years, he has spoken and consulted in various industries helping his clients improve their performance, productivity and profitability.

Since 2000, Ken has been one of only nine certified business process and systems coaches for General Motors worldwide.

Ken is a contributing author to "**Mentoring: The Most Obvious Yet Overlooked Key to Achieving More in Life than You Ever Dreamed Possible,**" and "**How to Manage One Million Dollars Or Less.**" His first book, *"Your Better Self: A Simple Guide to Where You Want to Be,"* was published in 2009.

A professional member of the National Speakers Association since 1989, he is also a member of the Global Speakers Federation.

He can be reached at ken@YourBetterSelf.com. Visit YourBetterSelf.com and BetterThanYourBest. com to find more practical resources to help you be *your* better Self. Go to KenWallaceCompany. com to learn more about how Ken can help you and your organization increase your impact and significance in the world and to sign up for his free newsletter, *"Better Than Your Best."*

DEDICATION

As I did the book, "Your Better Self: A Simple Guide to Where You Want to Be," I dedicate this Self-Study Manual to the memory of my parents, Orlen and Helen Wallace, and to my wife, Dr. Mary Wallace, PhD, all three of whom have been instrumental in helping me experience my better Self. They have done this through consistently demonstrating selfless love, forgiveness and encouragement and by modeling the many inspiring attributes of their own better Selves.

FOREWORD

What are your worthy aspirations? If you can't answer this question immediately and exuberantly, you really don't know what they are yet. But you do have them. This self-study manual will help you identify and manifest all of your worthy aspirations. It will assist you to swiftly and easily access the tremendous resources of your better Self that will bring into your life everything you need—and want.

By the way, do you know what you want your life to be? What do you want to experience on a daily basis? Happiness, fame, wealth, power, recognition, peace of mind? Perhaps all of these—and more? You can never experience even one of these until you have marshaled the means of your better Self. This study manual, designed to delve deep into your self, will help you realize the depths beyond your operational consciousness. It will help you clarify your aspirations and then concentrate your "hidden" resources to manifest them all in your daily life.

Praise for Ken Wallace's work:

Russell Brunson, Founder and CEO of the internationally acclaimed, DotComSecrets, said this about my book, "Your Better Self: A Simple Guide to Where You Want to Be:"

> *"A powerful blueprint for how to courageously break through the clutter of adult life. This book is full of insight and inspiration to help you accomplish what is most important, overcome the things that aren't, and finally get things done in order to become all that you are meant to be."*

He extends his testimony of the book to this manual, as well.

Pieter Coetzer, CEO, Penta Securities in Bloemfontein, South Africa writes:

> *"It has been my privilege to know Ken Wallace for almost twenty years. There is a wonderful congruence between the man I know and the content of his book, 'Your Better Self: A Simple Guide to Where You Want to Be,' and now his 'Your Better Self Study Manual.'*
>
> *Ken really lives this book. And this book will make a big difference in the life of every reader who uses the many pauses in the book to reach for the Better Self waiting to be revealed in every one of us.*
>
> *What I like best is the way Ken guides you step by step to learn to like yourself and then to allow change to come into your life so you can be 'better than your best.' This book*

powerfully echoes Gandhi when he says, 'you must be the change you want to see in the world.'"

Charlie Brown, CEO, HBA, Inc. enthusiastically states:

> *"An outstanding book of uncommon wisdom gleaned from everyday, common experience. It helped me see myself in a different way than I had ever done before. I like what I see!"*

This guide was created to accompany you on your journey toward your better Self. I call it a "self study" manual because it will help you unite the many parts of your examined self into a whole that brings to bear its immense strength, focus and power to flesh out all of your worthy aspirations. Then you'll find yourself living on purpose in peace and prosperity for the rest of your life.

Your better Self eagerly awaits your arrival.

PREFACE

When you meet your better Self you'll immediately know your true capabilities to live the life you really want. When you embrace your better Self you will successfully transform into the person you want to be.

"Your Better Self" books guide you to manifesting your worthy aspirations. They reveal the inner resources available to you right now that will help you make them real. They offer uplifting and motivational content designed to inspire you to move immediately in the direction of your waking dreams.

This self-study manual, when used together with the book, will help you accomplish more, be more confident, worry less, overcome your fears and experience more peacefulness in your life. They provide specific and practical ways to get in touch with your better Self.

Use this handbook for successful implementation to achieve any goal and possess anything that is worthy of you. Then share them with others in your life whom you wish to see do better than their best at manifesting all their worthy aspirations. When you live within a community of better Selves, life takes on new meaning and deeper significance.

Self-study makes you worthy of receiving the benefits of living as your better Self. When you study, you spend time with yourself and you become more intimately acquainted with the truth about you—of what you're capable of being, doing and having.

There is no shame in studying yourself. It is the way to explore your heart, mind and soul so that you can know precisely what you want, how to get it and how to share it. Your better Self comprises the "infinity of possibility" that yearns to be explored.

As you explore with the help of this guide, you'll find everything you need to live a peaceful, whole and prosperous life. In fact, you'll discover that you already had everything you needed at the start. But now you can use it in more powerful, focused and innovative ways to create the reality you really want to live in.

You become worthy of your aspirations and they become worthy of you when you study your self and learn the ways you can live as your better Self.

INTRODUCTION

This manual is designed to be used as a compliment to and in conjunction with my book, *"Your Better Self: A Simple Guide to Where You Want to Be."* It can most certainly be read by itself as a proper book in its own right. However, there are allusions and references to content in the book such that some of the content of this manual might appear incomplete.

The purpose of the book is to offer scenarios and stories—slices of real life—so that readers can "self-identify" the specific areas of life they need to work on so they can increase their motivation and energy to straightforwardly manifest their worthy aspirations and more quickly become their better Selves. The purpose of this manual is to be a companion to the book, offering additional content, stories, resources, tools and exercises to help readers delve more deeply into those areas of opportunity to improve themselves. Taken together, the book and this manual provide all that is needed to more rapidly and easily become your better Self and get what you really want in your life.

How to Use This Manual

When you read a chapter in the book that beckons you to explore that particular theme of life at a deeper level, pick up this manual and go to that same chapter (the manual has the same chapter names and sequence as the book) and read the additional content. More importantly, be sure to do the exercises as these will help you get clearer on the specific and unique ways YOU can become YOUR better Self.

T. S. Eliot wrote, "Half of the harm that is done in this world is due to people who want to feel important . . . They do not mean to do harm . . . They are absorbed in the endless struggle to think well of themselves." The book and this manual are designed to help readers think well of themselves without the endless struggle and, by so doing, to live peacefully and productively as their better Selves.

Thank you for being a part of the growing "Your Better Self" community! I hope we meet at a Your Better Self Improvement seminar soon. For more information about the seminar, go to http:// YourBetterSelf.com/seminar.html.

What Does <u>YOUR</u> Better Self Look Like?

In the space below, draw a picture of your better Self. What are you doing? What are you looking at? What is your mood? What have you accomplished? What are you looking forward to? Are you in the process of manifesting your worthy aspirations? Are you enjoying the benefits of having already manifested them?

Don't have artistic skills? Not to worry. Your drawing is not about perfection—nor is it about having certain skills. It's about using what you have in creative ways. Don't be afraid of not being able to "perfectly" depict the inner picture you have of your better Self. It will only begin to become real after you've taken a single step—no matter how frivolous it might at first appear to be—to manifest it in the real world.

My better Self looks something like this:

"An aspiration is a joy forever, a possession as solid as a landed estate, a fortune which we can never exhaust and which gives us year by year a revenue of pleasurable activity."

—Robert Louis Stevenson

A Note About Thinking and Learning

Your brain is an amazing instrument that both processes and produces far more than you're consciousness allows you to perceive. The best way to become more aware of what your brain is up to is to "just" THINK. You don't need to plan your thoughts or even the subjects you will ponder. "Just think." See what happens. More often than not, you'll discover that you are your own best teacher about things you didn't know you already knew!

You Get What You Give

This maxim is as old as the proverbial "hills." But, like all platitudes and axioms, it has stood the test of time because it is true. You will receive value from this study manual to the degree you involve yourself and willingly participate in doing the exercises. What you give in the way of energy and effort in studying yourself, you will receive in greater understanding of and access to your better Self.

The chapter of the book, *"'Give Up' Giving,"* ends with this statement: *"The key to abundant living, which exemplifies your better Self, is abundant giving beyond your selfish need to give."* In other words, what you give without expectation of receiving anything in return is what you'll get in abundance. **How** you give is perhaps even more important than **what** you give.

Give yourself the gift of self-examination. When you do, your better Self joins with your worthy aspirations to produce a life of purpose, power, peace, productivity and prosperity.

Socrates was right: *"The unexamined life is not worth living."* Neither is it worthy living. It is not worthy of your better Self. This manual will help you properly and thoroughly examine your life so that its worth exceeds your wildest imaginings and produces significantly improved results in your daily living.

Questions and Answers

The following words of the poet Rainer Maria Rilke have helped me "stay the course" toward the Answers I seek by remaining steadfast in the Questions so I can more clearly comprehend precisely what I am asking of life.

> *"Be patient toward all that is unsolved in your heart and try to love the Questions themselves. Do not now seek the Answers which cannot be given you because you would not be able to live them and the point is to live Everything. Live the Questions now. Perhaps you will gradually, without noticing, live along some distant day into the Answer."*
> Rainer Maria Rilke (1875-1926).

This self-study manual will help you live and love the Questions of your life so you can come to a better understanding of what you are asking and what you are expecting of your life. Your Questions are your aspirations. Some of the Answers will be given; others will remain elusive, yet, perhaps become clearer in their implications for the way you choose to live from now on.

Foundational Principle

The foundational principle of this self-study manual is simple: you have enormous resources present within you to live on purpose in peace and prosperity but you don't know how to easily and quickly access these resources because of the way you think of yourself now. The book, ***"Your Better Self: A Simple Guide to Where You Want to Be"*** and this self-study manual will help you think better of yourself so you can become and perform better than your current "best" in everything you do.

COMMITTING TO YOUR JOURNEY

The creation of your better Self won't just happen. It will require, as its first prerequisite, a quality that is ALREADY INSIDE YOU called commitment. But what is commitment, and how can you activate it, so that it becomes your **personal** commitment, and will begin to guide you on your journey?

First, you should know precisely what the word means. According to the *Oxford American Dictionary*, it is described as "the state of being involved in an obligation" and is defined as "an obligation or pledge." But in the everyday parlance of speech, it can mean several very different things when it takes the form of an action word, or verb. People are said to "commit" crimes or sins, to be "committed" to institutions, to "commit" to relationships, to "commit" atrocities or adultery.

When you are committed to a bad practice, you set up problematic patterns for your future relationships with others—both casual and intimate. Conversely, committing yourself to positive practices yields healthy patterns that result in deeply satisfying and mutually fulfilling relationships, enabling you to accomplish more than you ever could alone or while in the midst of a stressful relationship.

The common thread of all the forms that the word "commitment" takes is to decide, to make a decision, and then to comport your behavior accordingly. Your actions flow from your decisions such that the resulting outcomes make your commitment a reality. Few ideas, plans or dreams ever become realities without committing yourself to making them so.

In the context of *Your Better Self*, another consideration immediately becomes: Am I worthy of committing? You may consider yourself unworthy, undeserving, because of decisions you have made in the past. But do bad decisions you've committed to once actually disqualify you from committing to begin the construction of *your better Self* NOW, in the current moment, as you're reading this?

Before you commit to anything, you should know precisely what you're committing to. The "better you" is not a "best you," because the word "best" implies a limit that is self-imposed, and which assumes that you have reached your zenith, the peak of your aspirations, of what you can be. If you achieve a "best" you before you die, that doesn't leave much room for improvement, does it?

Still, you will need to form in your mind's eye some grand vision of this "better you"—a precise "picture" of what you would like to become and how you would like to consistently behave. For any of us, this type of envisioning is a project—something you will have to assemble piece-by-piece, bit-by-bit. It doesn't just happen. It will happen one tiny commitment at a time.

When you begin any job, it takes the right tools. Recently, I was attempting to change the ink cartridge in my favorite pen. I firmly shoved it into the pen's casing only to discover that it was too big. No matter how hard I pulled, I couldn't remove the cartridge. I tried twisting, yanking . . . yelling! Nothing worked. Then I thought of using pliers. That was it! I needed the right tool for the job. I retrieved a pair of pliers from a drawer in the kitchen and grasped the cartridge while pulling with my fingers on the end of the casing.

After several futile attempts, all I succeeded in doing was to dent the cartridge. I had about given up when it occurred to me to use another pair of pliers instead of my fingers. With two pliers I gently pulled the cartridge from the casing as easy as you please. Sometimes, what you commit to requires multiple tools to make it happen. Not just any tools—the RIGHT tools. The most effective tools for the job of becoming—and remaining—your better Self are mental in nature. They are the ways you think, reflect, remember, choose and imagine.

To find your better Self you will need a probe or mirror to see inside yourself. We call that mirror "introspection." So your first tool will be using introspection to examine the inner recesses of your soul—to explore not just what *is*, but what *was*—as the "you" that you are at this moment came to be. For many people who are not used to using this tool to see inside themselves, this first tool will have to be sharpened.

Developing Introspection

Most people are not introspective while they're living their lives. They think, although this is not really true, that they are "too busy living their lives" to "get lost in introspection." Some of you might "think back" and get lost in **retrospection**, ruminating about the past, and wishing that **if only** you'd done something different *way back when*—then your life would be "just peachy" in the present-tense. While retrospection can be an aid in finding your path to introspection, it is NOT the same as introspection.

> **Exercise 1**: Look up the words introspection and retrospection in your favorite dictionary. What are the differences you can find that help you better understand why your first tool to finding your better Self is NOT retrospection? How do you think introspection will help you get to know yourself better?
>
> _____
> _____
> _____
> _____
> _____
> _____

> **Exercise 2**: Practice reflecting about the person most involved in raising you. Was that person generally happy? Had they created their "better Self" while you knew them? Why? Why not? Could you have changed anything about yourself that would have changed that person into their "better Self?" Would anything that you could have done at the time really have made a significant difference?

_____
_____
_____
_____
_____
_____

It is very unlikely that you, as a child, especially as a small child, could have done anything that might have, in and of itself, created their "better Self." But many of us feel guilt over such "what ifs, could haves, and should haves." Sometimes that guilt can be crippling, like a wound oozing pus inside your mind. What wounds have been oozing their poison into your mind over the years? Who inflicted those wounds on you? Who is doing it now? If the wounds are still oozing, why haven't they healed yet? Remember what you're mother told you: "If you don't stop picking that scab, it will never heal!"

> **Exercise 3**: "In every adult lies the child that was, and in every child lies the adult that will be." If you are an adult (or consider yourself to be), how would you describe the child that lies within you today? If you are a child, how would you describe the adult within you that is being fashioned by what you're thinking and doing today?

_____
_____
_____
_____
_____
_____

Retrospection, if used singly, is not a road to introspection. Too often, it becomes a one-way path to negative emotions, such as guilt and remorse, which can stifle any hope of replenishing your energy and desire to create and experience a "better you." If you look backwards, you should have some idea of what you're looking for. The Danish philosopher, Soren Kierkegaard, said, "Life can only be understood backwards; but it must be lived forwards." What do you think this means in terms of committing yourself to becoming your better Self and helping others become their better Selves?

_____
_____
_____
_____
_____
_____
_____
_____

Sir Winston Churchill said, "The farther backward you can look, the farther forward you are likely to see." How far back are you looking to see what *else* your past might mean for your future?

The past, contrary to popular belief, is not set in stone. In fact, whenever we recall a past experience we are often conflating a variety of recollections and putting them together along the path of previous interpretations and assigned meanings. This is why the past seems inflexible and static.

Furthermore, interpretations and meanings of past events are not limited to ours alone. Other people's intpretations of a shared experience often substitue for our own because we have accepted their narrative as more meaningful than ours. In other words, we let others tell the story of our history. This happens when we don't spend enough serious time exploring other meanings our memories can have. Your better Self will remain trapped in a dimensionless past and an unfamiliar history until you commit to mining your memories for multiple meanings. When you do, your better Self is able to see forward much farther—and much more clearly.

Aside from potentially zooming in on the negative, retrospection can also do the opposite: zoom in on the positive. If your goal is to look backward and to arrive at a pleasant, fun time, you will also be tempted to stay there—in that comfortable place. But the secret to self-examination is to find the REAL you, which in actuality contains elements of positive and negative, yin and yang, good and bad. Self-examination is a lot more like introspection, but what it won't do, is allow you to stay in your comfort zone.

Introspection, and commitment, by the way—are all about taking you OUT of your comfort zone. When you commit to your journey it means putting yourself out there, stepping out—out of your comfort zone. After some reflection and self-examination, that is, introspection, you'll be prepared to take that crucial step with confidence and boldness.

Exercise 4: What have you committed to lately? It could be an activity, a person, your pet, maintenance of a car or truck, or just about anything specific that you have in mind. If you can't think of anything, then DECIDE to commit right now to one single thing. What is that thing? Do you believe you have it "in you" to make a commitment to make it real in your life?

_____
_____
_____
_____
_____
_____

A Deeper Dive

Let's look at another dictionary's definition of commitment. The *Merriam-Webster Dictionary* states that commitment is: *a: an agreement or pledge to do something in the future;* **b:** *the state or an instance of being obligated or emotionally impelled.*

Emotion plays an integral part in making any commitment—and keeping it. By its very nature, commitment involves looking to the future and imagining a better situation than you're experiencing currently. How you feel about that situation and whether or not you truly believe it will be "better" is a primary factor in committing your personal resources to making it so.

You will encounter obstacles and difficulties in your journey of commitment. You will be tempted to doubt yourself, your very abilities and desire to accomplish your better future and arrive at your better Self. Your feelings of worthiness of a better future sometimes waiver just as you embark on the journey.

But when doubt is your travel companion it doesn't have to be your enemy. Rather, it can be a great source of strength. Rollo May remarked, "The relationship between commitment and doubt is by no means an antagonistic one. Commitment is healthiest when it is not without doubt but in spite of doubt." At the heart of any commitment is this motto: *"If I believe I can achieve it, and begin it, I'll do it—in spite of any and all obstacles."*

It's true: the most important factor in your success is commitment. Commitment ignites action. It means to pledge yourself to behave in certain ways according to certain principles in a consistent manner. You must manifest a sound set of beliefs that have at their base the ardent desire to help others become their better Selves. Steadfast adherence to those beliefs results in being able to tap into your unseen resources that help to complete your commitments. Persistence with purpose defines the pattern of conduct that leads to your better Self.

The Power of Getting Started

Getting started on your journey of commitment takes the first step. Once taken, it starts movement in the direction of your aspirations. It creates the will and the willpower to take the next step. Goethe said it best: "Whatever you can do, or dream you can do, begin it. Boldness has genius and power and magic in it."

There is immense power in action. Taking action can get you moving with surprising momentum but you must be certain that the direction you start off in is the one you want to maintain with equal enthusiasm. Otherwise, the great start will fizzle and the momentum will slow to a halt while leaving you to feel badly about having tried and failed to do something to improve yourself.

Where do you want to go? What do you want to be? What must you do to start getting there? Take that step—NOW! Do it before you continue reading or before you do anything after you've stopped reading! Do it now. Seriously.

Don't have a clue what to commit to that will make your Self and your future better? Here are ten suggestions. Any of these will be worthy of your time and effort to incorporate them into your personal commitments:

1. A set of values, principles, beliefs. These define your uniqueness and the fundamental direction you would like to go in life.

2. Commit to yourself and how you act on a daily basis. Focus on integrity, honesty, confidence, accountability and transparency. Willingly acknowledge the part others play in your success. Strive for continuous personal improvement.

3. Prioritize your goals and identify specifically what your top three worthy aspirations are that you ardently desire to regularly experience; in other words, what kind of person do you want to become and what does that person do on a daily basis?

4. The more you give the more you receive. If what you give is negative, that's what you'll get back. Likewise, if what you give is positive and constructive you will receive more than what you'll ever need to continue to be your better Self. The improvement of others is key to the improvement of yourself. Commit to providing what others need from you to become their better Selves.

5. Gird yourself for the long haul. Commitment only yields its fruits after effort is expended over a period of time. *"Stick-to-it-ive-ness"* is the key to experiencing the benefits of your commitments. True commitment stands the test of time.

6. Communication is paramount to successfully completing your commitments. Whatever does not create clarity contributes to ambiguity and confusion. Focus on saying what you mean and meaning what you say. Simple, yet powerful.

7. Concentrate on adding value in all your relationships and call attention to what is working. Lead by example. Support and defend those who support your efforts and intentions; stand up to those whose words and/or actions demonstrate disrespect of your commitments and who seek to undermine them.

8. Look for better ways to make decisions. Eliminate complacency and confront what is not working. Challenge your current expectations and actively seek to make positive changes in the ways you interact with others.

9. Focus on optimism for the future not dissatisfaction with the past or disillusionment with the present. When Professor Porsche was asked which was his favorite model of the many Porsche automobiles, he quipped, "I haven't built it yet!" Your future will be better to the extent that you want it to be. It will become better when you become your better Self.

10. How you weather the tempests of suffering and the trials of misfortune most clearly demonstrates your commitment to your values and principles. Epicurus wrote that " . . . a captain earns his reputation during the storms." It is most difficult to adhere to your commitments when faced with stiff resistance and conflict. It is easiest to compromise your commitments during these times.

➢ Which one of these ten suggestions will help you most to make and keep your commitments to manifest your worthy aspirations and become your better Self?

_____

_____

_____

_____

_____

_____

_____

_____

Exercise 5: Ask yourself, "If I pay the price of staying true to my commitments, what do I think the benefits might be? Are they worth the cost of enduring strong opposition, resistance and/or confrontation?" If you don't believe they are, then your commitment will wane and the results you say you want won't ever materialize.

_____

_____

_____

_____

_____

_____

When your commitments are met with derision, disregard, disrespect and disgust—even aggressive attacks, what can you do to keep faith with your commitments to become your better Self?

Wally Amos, founder of "Famous Amos Cookies," was a featured speaker at one of the national conventions of the National Speakers Association. During his speech, he quoted a poem that intrigued me about the strength of character that the courage of commitment provides. After the convention, my family and I were waiting with Wally at the airport to catch the same plane to St. Louis. I asked him if he would send me a copy of that poem which he did promptly upon his return home to Hawaii.

"Do It Anyway!"
(Attributed, variously, to Dr. Kent M. Keith and Sal Sperlinsa)

"People are unreasonable, illogical and self-centered—love them anyway!
If you do good, people will accuse you of selfish ulterior motives—do good anyway!
If you are successful, you will win false friends and true enemies—succeed anyway!
The good you do today will be forgotten tomorrow—do good anyway!
Honesty and frankness make you vulnerable—be honest and frank anyway!
The biggest people with the biggest ideas can be shot down by the smallest people with the smallest minds—think big anyway!
People favor underdogs but follow only top dogs—fight for some underdog anyway!

What you spend years building may be destroyed overnight—build anyway!
People really need help but may attack you if you help them—help people anyway!
Give the world the best you've got and you'll get kicked in the teeth—give the world the best you've got anyway!"

A final stanza has been added along the way, attributed to Mother Theresa, which sums up the entire poem:

"You see, in the final analysis, it is between you and God—it was never between you and them anyway!"

Exercise 6: What does the poem, "Do It Anyway!" mean to you? Does it describe—at least to some extent—your current situation? How?

_____
_____
_____
_____
_____
_____

Today, someone is looking at you as a role model for how they should live their lives. What "model" are you giving them to follow? If they followed your example, would it make you happy and proud of them?

What are some things you can do to stay on the "high road" when the going gets tough and you're feeling all alone in your journey?

_____
_____
_____
_____
_____
_____

Do it anyway! Yes, you **can** do it . . . anyway . . . regardless of any obstacles you may be experiencing at the moment. Keep in mind the famous quote from Henry Ford: *"If you think you can or can't—you're right."* Believe you can make—and keep—your commitments. Embody the words of the People's Poet, Edgar A. Guest:

"Somebody said that it couldn't be done.
But he with a chuckle replied,
That 'maybe it couldn't' but he would be one
Who wouldn't say no till he tried.
So he buckled right in with a trace of a grin
On his face. If he worried he hid it.

He started to sing as he tackled the thing
That couldn't be done, and he did it."

Exercise 7: Have you ever tried something new when you weren't sure you'd succeed at doing it—maybe because everyone said it couldn't be done? How did you feel when you started? How did you feel when you tackled the thing that couldn't be done—and you did it? What caused you to start it . . . and finish it? How do you think you were able to do it?

_____

_____

_____

_____

_____

_____

The Power of Having Started

D. H. Murray, leader of the 1930's Scottish Himalayan Expedition, did an outstanding job defining commitment and its consequences:

> *"Until one is committed, there is hesitancy—a chance to draw back; always ineffectiveness. Concerning all acts of initiative and creation, there exists one elementary truth the ignorance of which kills limitless ideas and splendid plans: that the moment one commits oneself, then providence moves, too. All sorts of things occur to help one that would never otherwise have occurred. A whole stream of events issues from the decision, raising in one's favor all manner of unforeseen incidence and meetings and material assistance which no one could have dreamt would have come his/her way."*

Patanjali expressed similar themes many centuries earlier (second century, B.C.) when he wrote:

> *"When you are inspired by some great purpose, some extraordinary project, all your thoughts break their bounds: your mind transcends limitations, your consciousness expands in every direction and you find yourself in a new, great and wonderful world. Dormant forces, faculties and talents become alive, and you discover yourself to be a greater person by far than you ever dreamed yourself to be."*

In the *Psychology of Power*, J. A. Hadfield observed, *"We lead timid lives shrinking from difficult tasks until perhaps we are forced into them and immediately we seem to unlock our unseen forces."*

➤ How are you shrinking today from difficult tasks?

_____

_____

_____

_____

_____

_____

➢   Are D. H. Murray's comments true for you? How about the words of Patanjali? How?

_____

_____

_____

_____

➢   What are YOUR "unseen" and "dormant" forces?

_____

_____

_____

_____

_____

➢   What is your "tipping point"—your commitment to manifesting a worthy aspiration—that is inspiring you to become your better Self . . . today?

_____

_____

_____

_____

_____

_____

There is great power and energy already within us ready to be tapped in the service of manifesting our worthy aspirations. Commitment is the tipping point that "forces" us into accessing them and using them in surprising ways. In fact, once commitment causes us to take the first step, all kinds of resources and "unseen forces" we never thought of before come to aid us in becoming our better Selves.

YOU HAVE WHAT IT TAKES

Commitment takes courage. William James, founder of American psychology, defined courage not as the opposite of cowardice, but as the opposite of conformity. He also said, "Act as if what you do makes a difference. It does." In other words, you have what it takes.

We do conform most of the time, because like water coursing down a hill and seeking its level, it's easier—although for water the act of draining is crafted by natural laws. For people, the act of conforming is often intentional, sometimes even an intellectual action. We choose to follow the crowd because we think so many people can't be wrong. But even applauded American virtues such as "self-reliance" and "individuality" can become a source of conformity to the degree we adhere to them while shunning the common sense of prevailing perspectives.

Blind conformity leads to thoughtless uniformity. What is a uniform? It is clothing that removes the distinctions and personal preferences of those who wear them. It shrouds each wearer in sameness such that uniqueness, although not erased, is minimized in importance and significance.

Conformity limits you to sets of approved choices. But who approves of these choices? It is important to know that, no matter who else approves of your choices, if YOU don't approve, you'll make choices that will end with undesired, perhaps detrimental consequences. This will not make you—or anyone else—happy (even if they do initially approve of your choice).

> **Exercise 1**: Consider your life as of this moment. Make a list of five things that you conform to, along with your neighbors, friends, or family. For example, do you live in a house? You are conforming. Do you drive a car or a pick-up truck? You are conforming. Do you go to school or send your children to school? You are conforming. Do you vote in elections or hope to when you're of age? You are, or will be conforming. In what ways does your conformity enhance your life? In what ways docs it hamper your life?

> _____
> _____
> _____
> _____
> _____
> _____

Conformity is not an evil in and of itself. A great deal of conformity is necessary for our society to function. But some conformity is merely arbitrary, pursued because of peer pressure or due to limits we impose upon ourselves that aren't really necessary, even if "approved by the many." A full obeisance to every possible tenet of conformity available to your experience is like imposing a wall of "*I must do this*!" between you and your "sky," in the sense that your sky is a symbol of your aspirations—your highway to a "better you."

Don't overdo conformity! Try to examine and review every decision you make with a stray musing or two. Next time you hear someone say, "The sky's the limit!" you'll know that to be true only to the extent that you refuse to allow your choices to be directed by your desire to be part of the crowd. Otherwise, your limit will be far lower than the sky.

You DON'T want your choices to relegate your life to an existence built upon "comfortable misery." To prevent this from happening, you have to develop your abilities to discern when to conform—and as William James might imply—when NOT to.

We like to tout the innocence of children because they begin as a blank slate and as they grow older and learn about who they are and about the environments they must adapt to, it is sometimes amusing for adults to observe this process in action. But the innocence of children is lost not only when they are compelled into making poor decisions, but also and perhaps more sadly when they allow themselves to become *predictable*. A child who is too predictable has had their innocence stolen from them, stolen by a ritualized conformity, and often when this occurs, the consequences are tragic.

> **Exercise 2**: What are some penalties you have experienced in life because you refused to conform? What are some penalties you have experienced in life because you DID conform? Do your family or friends exert pressure on you to be a certain way that they find acceptable? How does this make you feel? Can you ever be your better Self when you conform to the expectations that others impose upon you? Is it possible to be your better Self if you constantly rebel against others' reasonable expectations of you?

_____
_____
_____
_____
_____
_____

Conformity, and receiving acceptance by others, is very important in determining how we perceive ourselves. Our self-image in many cases *depends* upon such acceptance. But is your current self-image relevant to you in the sense that it is all that will ever be? If it is, you'll NEVER become a better YOU.

Remember that courage is the opposite of conformity, and you didn't really need the ghost of William James to tell you that. You already knew it, because YOU HAVE WHAT IT TAKES to courageously commit to becoming your better Self. You have what it takes because you can commit to manifesting your worthy aspirations regardless of what others think. Which brings us to . . .

YOUR BIGGEST OBSTACLE

What is the bump in the road that you're facing as you drive in a new direction while creating your better Self—in other words, a better YOU? It's your concern about what other people think of you.

We like to be seen in a favorable light. It makes sense. If everyone you know has an unfavorable perception of YOU, you probably feel a bit like the proverbial deer caught in the headlights. While a deer can't feel shame except if it's a cartoon character like Rudolf the red-nosed at Christmas time (and anyway, he doesn't really count because he's a *reindeer*), people can experience a smorgasbord of "lousy" emotions when the "headlights" of unfavorable scrutiny are suddenly fixed on them.

> **Exercise 1**: Imagine something you're engaged in with other people going awry. It could be an activity you enjoy, or maybe not. Go there in your mind's eye. You've just messed up and people are looking at YOU. What are some of the emotions you're feeling? How are you dealing with them? Could you deal with them better? How?

As you've already read, it takes courage to NOT conform. But if you'd wanted to conform, and by accident failed to conform, that's a lot different than if you'd made a commitment not to conform, if it was your conscious decision to "follow a different drumbeat." If you choose to make a better you out of yourself, people are eventually going to notice. That scrutiny can be exhilarating, or it can be excruciating. Which it is depends on the level of your confidence in your commitment.

We also perceive ourselves as unique. Often we assume—incorrectly—that even the humdrum versions of ourselves are "special" to those around us. An egotistical selfishness is at the root of this "I'm special" attitude. When we're in this remote control mode, we can bulldoze the feelings of those around us as if they were satellites in our own orbit, and we are the controlling planet. Once in a while, this kind of attitude "works," but more often it doesn't. At any rate, if you're content with this humdrum "special" you, why bother changing into a new and improved model? Thankfully, there IS a way around this conundrum.

The best way that your better Self, in other words, your better YOU, can express its own uniqueness is by bringing out the uniqueness of OTHERS. Instead of thinking of yourself or what others think of you, you can choose to think of others. If you do this consciously, there's also a bonus coming to you: suddenly, you'll find yourself surrounded by better Selves who are more likely to perceive YOU in a positive light. They will also be more likely to help you in your efforts to become your better Self.

But it has to happen spontaneously, as an indirect result of your ACTIONS. Your better Self is not concerned about what others think because YOU are too busy becoming a better YOU by helping others become their better Selves.

Another tip about human nature: People don't really think about you that often. In fact, tests conducted at the "University of Common Sense" have revealed conclusively that other people hardly ever think about you—unless something brings you to mind. Without that essential trigger, it hardly ever happens—certainly not enough for you to have to worry about.

> **Exercise 2**: Think about someone you haven't thought about in a long time. Do you think they know you're thinking about them right now? Do they care? Do you? Who do you know who is thinking about you right this very moment? How do you know they're thinking of you? Could they be thinking of something or somebody else instead of you? Why would they be thinking of you and not anything else right now? What does it matter if they are—or aren't thinking of you right now?

_____
_____
_____
_____
_____
_____

You now have the mental tools to overcome your biggest obstacle to becoming your better Self. You had them all along, didn't you?

THE "GIDDY-UP" METHOD OF SELF MOTIVATION

"GIDDY-UP" to a better you. Your better Self is just a couple of hoof beats away with each letter in my method spurring you along. Get along little humans! Get along! "Get along" is the "technical" definition of "Giddy Up!" don't you know.

G is for **Get**, I is for **It**, D is for **Done by** (giving yourself the best motivating gift of all—a deadline), a second D is for **Determining**, Y is for **Your**, U is for **Unique**, P is for **Purpose**. The point is that you have to be self-motivated. You have to motivate yourself to move in a specific direction. If you divide the word "motivation" in two, you could come up with a good definition: a **"motive" to take "action."** Your drive, your impetus, your motion forward toward your aspirations must come from inside you, not from some external stimuli.

Worthy aspirations don't just happen. They can never be free-floating or unrealistic unless you've chosen for them to remain fantasies. If your aspirations remain tethered to the realm of the daydream, then they'll always be pipedreams. You have to choose to make your aspirations real—by linking them to a determined sense of purpose—by purposely pursuing them. GIDDY-UP!

> **Exercise:** What do you aspire to? Think of something worthy of you. Is this something you ache to achieve? What will you need to do to make your aspiration happen? How will you prepare?

_____

_____

_____

_____

_____

Preparation means to contemplate and mentally configure a future desired state. Preparation is the secret that will make your GIDDY-UP possible. Prepare to become your better Self by designing your future with the uniqueness of your purpose for living. Why are you alive? Why do you want to continue to be alive? You are unique and your presence in the world creates a reality that could never be what it is without you.

What do you do now? Get clear on your motives for taking action to create your better future. Will achieving what you say you want be a worthy expression of your unique purpose for living? GIDDY-UP!

FINDING HOME

Andrew recalled the house where he grew up with his sister Suzie. The number of the house was ten. It was marked with two huge numbers—a one and a zero—on the front door. It had been many years since he had visited his childhood home. He feared he had forgotten most everything about it—except the street number. His mother lived there all her life, and died there. His cat Floozie also lived there, an angora feline, and she might still live there for all Andrew knew. Can you help Andrew find his way home?

How could you help Andrew? Perhaps the first step would be to help him understand what the number ten symbolizes to him. When he thinks of the number ten, what comes to his mind? What memories are evoked? How does he feel? His answers to these questions constitute Andrew's concept of "home." By asking him such questions, you are helping him find his way home.

When Andrew finally made a journey back to the town in which he grew up, he was amazed at how easily he remembered everything about his childhood home. He eventually realized that, although he had left his home many years ago, his home had never left him throughout that time. It was always within him, just a memory away, a thought of times gone by, intimating its presence at the tip of his mind because it was an integral part of his soul. From that moment on, Andrew found his way home wherever he went. Sometimes the means to find your way home was never really lost. It's the same with finding your better Self.

> **Exercise:** Why do you think Andrew wanted to find his way home? Is finding your way home a metaphor for finding your better Self? Why or why not? Where is YOUR home? Are you there or are you trying to find your way there? Where are you now if you're not "at home?"

_____

_____

_____

_____

_____

_____

YOUR JOURNEY TOWARD EMPATHY

Empathy is the primary emotional expression of your better Self. Becoming your better Self involves journeying into deeper levels of what empathy means and, more particularly, what it looks and feels like when it is experienced.

Identifying with someone else—expressing empathy—is seldom easy. What is easy is our tendency to become self-absorbed. We get distracted with selfish concerns, and sometimes when we observe someone else's plight, even that's a distraction from our self-concern. When we notice someone else's needs, and feel a twinge of sympathy or even compassion, that is NOT empathy. To be empathic, our feelings must include a willingness to help that person—and then be converted into action. Prior to that action occurring, genuine empathy is never realized.

We tend to care more about, and empathize more easily with people who are more like us.

Exercise 1:

Scenario 1—A man's pet collie has run away. The owner of the dog, a neighbor you know and like, knocks on your door. You have also lost a cat during the past few months.

Scenario 2—A man's pet collie has run away. The owner of the dog, a stranger you've never met, knocks on your door. You don't like dogs, especially collies.

Who are you likely to have more empathy for? Do we have a choice in who we can feel empathy for?

_____
_____
_____
_____
_____
_____

The true challenge is to help *either* person.

How can you develop more empathy for more people in your life—even those whom are not like you and whom you do not like?

It might help to have a personal board of advisors—five people you trust—to help you discover the empathy that resides in the better you. Get their phone numbers, and have these at the ready. Who are these people? Write their names down now.

Name: **Tel. Number:**

_____   _____

_____   _____

_____   _____

_____   _____

_____   _____

You should not just use this intimate network as a "gossip" venue, but use these trusted persons to explore issues that occur which *might* require empathy. Tell these people in your network about your plans to become more empathetic and helpful to others as you progress toward a better you.

The basic inclination of many people, when approached in this manner, is to offer help and encouragement. This is what you need. Ask for it. Give people a chance to say "yes." Don't worry if they say "no," because, if they do, you'll have a chance to express empathy by asking how you can help them—even if they won't help you!

In your conversations you'll want to ask specific questions about the topic at hand. It will be most conducive to success if each conversation with the people in your group builds upon the previous one.

> **Exercise 2**: Identify one person with whom you are not getting along. Think about the reasons why your relationship with that person is not good. What can help you better understand why this person is behaving toward you as he/she does—and why you behave toward him/her the way you do? Can you imagine any situation in which you would be willing to actually help this person if they needed your help?

_____

_____

_____

_____

_____

You might discover that a door has been opened by a greater appreciation for and practice of empathy—letting in your better Self.

"Give Up" Giving

We often hear about "giving" to a cause, as in making a donation or pledge. We get solicited frequently about how this cause or that charity or some not-for-profit needs your "support," which is almost invariably a request for funding.

Sometimes we sincerely may want to "Save the Whales" or "Help the Homeless" or a crisis may arise when a natural or human-caused disaster creates urgency for massive and immediate assistance. If we feel a deep-set empathy for a particular cause, then "giving" is simply an extension of that empathy; it is the action that reveals and completes your empathy.

But too often "giving" to any cause that you get solicited for becomes an obligation, not something to arouse your better Self. Such giving might be something you feel coerced into doing—by social pressure, a guilty conscience, or because of a selfish desire on your part to be thought well of. You might be giving only because others are giving (conformity). You might feel you need to give, without feeling the need of the person or people you're giving to.

This is not only counterproductive; it can lead to anger, hostility or other feelings that can lead you AWAY from a better you. So when giving begins to feel like a "chore," it's time to **give up giving**. Giving up giving is giving up your selfish need to give as an act of self-satisfaction, self-gratification and self-aggrandizement. It is not giving up giving entirely, of course. It is, rather, re-establishing the link between why you give with how you give regardless of what it is that you give (money, time, material goods, etc.).

The most effective giving is always more about the *receiver* than the *giver*. "Give up giving" is an attitude about why you give.

> **Exercise 1**: Do you think that giving out of gratitude differs from giving out of guilt? Which would your better Self do regardless of what is given? Is giving $100.00 out of gratitude worth more than $100.00 given out of guilt? Why? Why do YOU give what you're giving now?

_____

_____

_____

_____

_____

_____

Exercise 2: Think of the charities or causes or other needs you currently are "giving" to. Which ones are really extensions of empathy that you genuinely feel? Which ones are you "giving" to which are making you feel exploited, to a greater or a lesser degree? Which ones are you "giving" to which are making you feel like you're exploiting them?

_____

_____

_____

_____

_____

_____

Exercise 3: If you can't give money to a cause or a person who is in need because you have no money to give, how else can you specifically demonstrate your empathy? If they need the money and you give something else, is this giving as good as money? In what ways can you give from your heart, not just from your hand? Would you give if no one knew you gave—including the Internal Revenue Service?

_____

_____

_____

_____

_____

_____

Exercise 4: You have a million dollars to give. How do you give it? To whom? Why?

_____

_____

_____

_____

_____

A SIMPLE QUESTION

You can ask yourself a simple question that will save you tons of time, worry, and effort. But first, let me ask you a few other questions:

Are you finding too many ways to say 'no'? When people ask you for help, or favors, or are merely seeking to spend time with you, are you ambivalent and evasive, as a rule? Are you too self-absorbed?

If you answered 'yes' to any of these questions, and if delaying tactics have been a staple of your interactive game plan, your path to a better you will be strewn with thorns or covered with molten lava (and you aren't wearing shoes!). Instead of putting people off, and sending mixed messages, you can put your shoes back on and walk more confidently along the path to your better Self simply by asking, *"How long will it take?"* Practice this approach with your friends, co-workers, and family members at every opportunity. The answers you'll receive will astonish you.

> **Exercise:** Think of situations in any given day when people may approach you for help or guidance. How often does this occur? Are you stressed out when merely contemplating who or when you'll be approached? What situations do you dread most? Why? If you impose a limit on the time demanded, will that alleviate at least some potential stress? How will setting time boundaries help you help others better? Will it help you better serve others whom you're not serving well now?

_____

_____

_____

_____

_____

_____

When you ask, "How long will it take?" you create the psychological framework within which focused and constructive conversations can occur. These don't take long at all. If the answer you receive indicates that it will take longer than a few minutes, you can make arrangements for future time together.

You'll discover that you'll be able to say 'yes' more often to others' request for your time and attention. How long it all takes will depend on whether or not you ask a simple question.

LET OTHERS HELP

Getting to know YOU is a challenge. To honestly learn to know the intricacies of the body-mind combination that comprises your essence takes a lifetime of "on-the-job" reflection and observation. To know who you are and what you are capable of doing is the most intriguing labor you could possibly be involved in; if your method is lacking it can also be the most frustrating.

While introspection is helpful in steady doses, you run the risk of self-absorption and eventual boredom. To be bored with yourself is not a pleasant state of being. To really get to know YOU, the observations and feedback of others is not merely a luxury, it's a necessity. Self-knowledge is often, if not necessarily always, enhanced by the aid, encouragement, and presence of other people.

Even if you are a successful hermit, recluse, or East Indian fakir, any self-knowledge that is gained becomes especially difficult to quantify. Without the mirror of other people to constantly reflect the better you that you are becoming, who is to say that you really are becoming a better you? You can't ever say for sure if the contemplation, introspection, and self-revelations are functional in YOUR life, or even genuine, if you have nothing current to compare them with.

While examples of this solitary method seem to have worked with historical personages (i.e. Gandhi & Jesus), what would have happened if Jesus had STAYED in the desert, not just for 40 days, but for the rest of his earthly life, totally ignoring others? It might have evoked the sound of one hand clapping. It takes two to clap; it takes more than you to become your better Self.

Solitariness is fine unless it leads to isolation. Excluding others from your life equals excluding valuable substance that is essential to becoming your better Self.

We have to share our lives with others to give it meaning and to better understand how we can become our better Selves.

> **Exercise:** Who has the potential to teach you something about YOUR better Self? Who can you show your better Self to and perhaps bring out their better Self? How can you do this? What is the first step you'll take to do this—*today*? How will this step be one taken by *your better Self*?

_____

_____

_____

_____

_____

_____

THE TRAGEDY OF GOAL RUSH

Americans have trouble sleeping. People of all ages are increasingly afflicted with insomnia and bouts of melancholy. But sometimes, people can feel tired even when they are well rested. For many of us, life can be overwhelming and stressful. Anxiety can set in. The phrase "panic attack" is now part of "life" for millions of Americans. Television commercials offer a constant stream of pharmaceutical remedies to cope with anxiety and depression.

But before you reach for the pills, consider that your ailment might be something else entirely. I have a name for it: **Goal Rush**. It's a pitiful condition bred by the need for constant stimulation. Americans must always be "on the go." Constantly rushing toward our goals in a frenzy of "business," which is the definition of "goal rush," is not the way to a better you.

While this pattern of behavior may seem typical when you observe those around you also leading lives of quiet desperation, it is NOT essential, especially for you. Choices accumulate and can lead to undesirable outcomes in your life. But you only live once, and if you decide to bring fundamental changes into your experience in order to bring about increased peace of mind, you _will_ become your better Self.

> **Exercise:** You need a "time out" sometimes. It is wise to practice slowing down, listening to your heartbeat and breathing. Stress reduction and relaxation techniques are perhaps the best remedy for combating "goal rush," along with a period of steady, consistent exercise.
>
> Stop reading right now and mentally quiet yourself. While sitting in a chair with your feet flat on the floor begin to listen for your heartbeat as it appears in the various parts of your body. Where is it the "loudest?" Do you think you can slow it down if you spent the next ten minutes trying to do so? Next, become aware of your breathing. Is it deep or shallow? Is the rhythm of your inhaling and exhaling regular and consistent? Or are you holding in your breaths in an attempt to "control" what is going on around you?

_____

_____

_____

_____

_____

There are nine primary categories and activities of life that you can begin to take more control over without "holding your breath." They are: *relaxation, body, exercise, leisure and fun, work, diet, communication and self-expression, spirituality and meditation, lifestyle and support system.* When you are in conscious control of these, your better Self is at work—and play!

Following is a self-assessment that will help you greatly improve your ability to manage "goal rush" and to experience success without stress. The purpose of this test is to increase your awareness of yourself. You can use this test to monitor your ongoing progress in reducing stress by taking it again in six months. The only importance of this number is to compare yourself to yourself.

Remember, you are in charge of charting your own destiny to becoming your better Self.

Holistic Health Test

Each statement is scored according to how often you can apply the given statement to your ***daily*** life:

100-80%	80-60%	60-40%	40-20%	20-0%
5	4	3	2	1

Next to each statement place a number from 5 to 1.

(a) Relaxation:

Today/6 Months

_____/_____   I am generally relaxed and unworried.
_____/_____   I sleep well and regularly.
_____/_____   I fall asleep easily without help.
_____/_____   I have no trouble getting up.
_____/_____   I take brief relaxation breaks.
_____/_____ **Total**

(b) Body:

Today/6 Months

_____/_____   I feel fit, energetic and healthy.
_____/_____   I take responsibility for illness.
_____/_____   My body feels flexible and youthful.
_____/_____   My weight and muscle tone are good.
_____/_____   I respond to my body when it needs special care.
_____/_____ **Total**

(c) Exercise:

Today/6 Months

_____/_____ I do vigorous exercise at least three times a week. i.e., jogging.
_____/_____ I do stretching and limbering daily.
_____/_____ I walk rather than drive whenever I can.
_____/_____ I work regularly at improving my fitness.
_____/_____ **Total**

(d) Leisure and Fun:

Today/6 Months

_____/_____ I have energy to use my free time creatively.
_____/_____ I feel free to simply have fun without a purpose.
_____/_____ I laugh freely and frequently.
_____/_____ It's easy for me to joke with others.
_____/_____ I don't take life seriously.
_____/_____ **Total**

(e) Work:

Today/6 Months

_____/_____ I enjoy my work to the fullest.
_____/_____ I feel fulfilled and appreciated.
_____/_____ I work a moderate number of hours, avoiding excess overtime.
_____/_____ My communications with co-workers are open and harmonious.
_____/_____ I experience very little anxiety or insecurity.
_____/_____ **Total**

(f) Diet:

Today/6 Months

_____/_____ I eat natural wholesome foods without additives.
_____/_____ I avoid junk foods. i.e., soda and candy
_____/_____ I eat slowly, chewing my food well.
_____/_____ I eat primarily grains, fresh fruits and vegetables.
_____/_____ I avoid stimulants. i.e., coffee, alcohol and drugs.
_____/_____ **Total**

(g) Communication and Self-Expression:

Today/6 Months

_____/_____ I communicate easily and openly with others.
_____/_____ I am comfortable with new people and groups.
_____/_____ I am a good listener.
_____/_____ I feel free to ask when I need love or caring.

_____/_____ I deal well with my own and other people's emotions.

_____/_____ **Total**

(h) Spirituality and Meditation:

Today/6 Months

_____/_____ Spirituality plays a role in my life.

_____/_____ I meditate or spend time in introspection.

_____/_____ I meet regularly with others for inspiration.

_____/_____ I have faith in a power other than myself.

_____/_____ I use prayer and affirmation as a healing tool.

_____/_____ **Total**

(i) Lifestyle and Support System:

Today/6 Months

_____/_____ I feel that my lifestyle supports my health and spiritual needs.

_____/_____ The people I spend my time with are kindred spirits and help me grow.

_____/_____ I do everything in my power to foster my own health and wellbeing.

_____/_____ I am always seeking new ways to grow.

_____/_____ My family life is peaceful and harmonious.

_____/_____ **Total**

By taking this test twice within six months you'll discover how what you have chosen to do to improve has actually helped. Resolve to change your attitudes and behaviors in ways that will enable you and others to affirm more frequently and with more confidence those statements that describe the way you want to live your life. When you can make these statements with ease on a daily basis, your better Self jumps for joy!

GIVE YOURSELF TIME

Time is the most important thing we have. We all have a certain amount, and then it is gone. But occasionally—perhaps frequently—we don't manage our time well. We figure incorrectly about how long something will take, or we enter into activities where we lose control of time expended in order to participate. Sometimes to please others, we make commitments that we really can't afford to make. Sometimes, it gets worse: we start doing some activity, but fail to allow enough time to do it well. The results can be humiliating if not downright disastrous.

Worse still . . . we don't allow sufficient time to clarify and realize our own aspirations and which ones are truly worthy of our time and effort. We might allow some time—just not *enough*.

You are a product of both the quantity and quality of time you give yourself to conduct your daily activities. Read that sentence again. It's true. Are you giving enough time to everything you do throughout the day to get them done with dignity, grace and satisfaction? You can, if you aren't now.

When we don't have enough time to do something well, and we're in the middle of doing it, we become anxious and fidgety. Suddenly our mindset, if not our task, becomes laden with obstacles. Any balance you may have felt begins to vanish along with the fleeting time. You may become curt with others and impatient, and cranky, as you suddenly are face-to-face with . . . "time deprivation." If you'd just allowed enough time . . . things would have been different . . . **better**. But who deprived you of your time? Did you really have less time than anybody else that day?

> **Exercise:** Take a piece of paper and draw a simple "T-Chart" on it (see the example below). At the top of the left column write for the header the following words: *"Tasks for Today."* At the top of the right column write, *"Time Required for Successful Completion Today."* The evening before, write down all the tasks you plan to complete by the end of the next day. To the right of each task write down the amount of time you think it should take to get it done well.
>
> Now, add fifteen minutes. I'm not kidding. You may want to add twenty minutes for bigger, more complex tasks that require input from others in order to complete them. At the end of the day, total the respective times for each completed task, then add all the times together to arrive at the grand total. What did you learn about "***enough time***?" Did you give yourself enough time? Did you have any time "left over?" If you follow my advice, your answer will always be, '***YES!***'

Tasks for Today	Time Required for Successful Completion Today

Ralph Waldo Emerson commented, "For the resolute and determined there is time and opportunity." When you give yourself enough time, you are honoring both your tasks and your ability to do them well to capitalize on the opportunity before you. This is characteristic behavior of your better Self.

IMPROVING YOUR RELATIONSHIPS

Sometimes we have to deal with people who aren't easy to deal with. Have you ever met someone who pushes the limits of your patience? Chances are you even deal with someone on a regular basis, an acquaintance, friend, or family member that tests your resolve to be kind and give everybody a chance to be nice. Some people have close relationships with people they don't *like*.

Sometimes, it can be best to excise that offending person (or persons) from your life, but this is a last resort. In certain cases, it might not even be practical to sever a relationship entirely. When you *must* interact with someone who tends to irk you, sometimes a simple conversation can make a difference. This direct approach, also referred to as honesty, can help to mediate or reconcile when annoying people don't realize that they are annoying. The notion is, if they know about their behavior, they can change it, or if you are triggering them, perhaps you can change yours.

But don't blame them as a major part of this conversation. Aggressively blaming someone for anything immediately summons a defensive, often angry, reaction. It is human nature to both blame and to react negatively when blamed (even if deserved). Blaming as a means to resolve a dispute or to manage another's irritating behavior means that you are refusing to entertain the possibility that you could be an integral part of the conflict. You could be a major contributor to your own negative feelings regarding this relationship. In what ways could you be contributing to the discord?

Your most valuable piece of information that might very well serve to soon soothe the dissension is your perspective on the other's behavior. It is this information you should bring to the other's attention as a first attempt to establish a more fruitful and beneficial mutual relationship.

Be an information bringer, not a blamer.

> **Exercise 1**: Have you ever blamed anybody for anything? Have you done so today? Think about it. You might think you haven't when, in fact, you have—it's just become such a habit of thought that you don't recognize when you do it. Think about it again. Even if you were 'right' to blame another, did it actually help?
>
> _____
> _____
> _____
> _____
> _____
> _____

Getting something "off your chest" is important to do. If you keep carrying the added weight of an unresolved issue, your progress toward your better Self will slow and your desire to manifest your worthy aspirations will diminish. Your drive to think better of yourself and do better than your previous best will dampen and eventually grind to a halt. Often, getting things off your chest will be sufficient to alleviate the stress in the relationship.

On the other hand, some people seem to enjoy making other people miserable. Human vultures of this type are also a bit like a pit viper with its heat-sensors. They know how to "get to you." Wherever vulnerability, self-doubt, and other weaknesses in your personality exist, they WILL find it.

When you're not with the person who "pushes your buttons," ask yourself, "Why does this person's behavior bother me? If you can be honest with yourself, you WILL learn why.

> **Exercise 2**: Who really bothers you? Why? Make a list; check it twice to find out who's naughty and nice in this relationship. You'll discover the true degree of your own culpability as well as more legitimate causes for the other's behavior.

> _____
> _____
> _____
> _____
> _____
> _____

You can react or respond to this offensive person. Yes, you do have a choice. You *always* have a choice. Sometimes the choice may be a painful one, or go against your "gut" instinct, but a choice WILL present itself.

> **Exercise 3**: How do you habitually react to people who really bother you? When you can answer this question honestly, you'll be well on your way to freeing yourself from the tyranny of the past. New approaches will appear that you never considered before. Be honest.

> You need to get beyond habitual reactions if you want to be a better you!

> _____
> _____
> _____
> _____
> _____
> _____

> **Exercise 4**: What might be motivating that person who really bothers you to continue their behavior? What are they getting out of it? What's their reward, or payoff? Once you know it, how can you use that information to shape your own perspective so that you can alter your behavior so that the other person might naturally alter theirs?

> _____
> _____
> _____

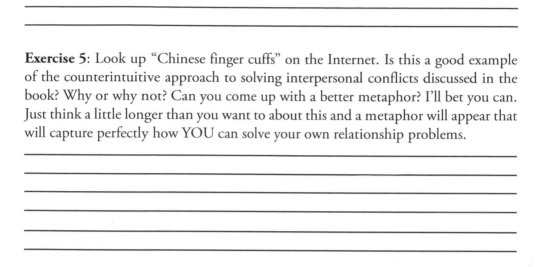

Exercise 5: Look up "Chinese finger cuffs" on the Internet. Is this a good example of the counterintuitive approach to solving interpersonal conflicts discussed in the book? Why or why not? Can you come up with a better metaphor? I'll bet you can. Just think a little longer than you want to about this and a metaphor will appear that will capture perfectly how YOU can solve your own relationship problems.

Resistance can produce increased resistance. Lack of resistance, especially when you *want* to resist, results in control over the extent you allow the irksome behavior of others to adversely impact your choices regarding how you will behave toward them. Improve your relationships by breaking the cycle of emotional and psychological resistance within them. This is what your better Self lives to do.

LOOK INTO YOUR OWN EYES

A photo of you reveals an aspect of your personality and appearance. A second photo, even one taken near the same time and in the same place, is likely to reveal something different. A third photo is likely to reveal something different than the first two, no matter how subtle. This process can continue indefinitely, especially if you've been photographed a lot.

Exercise 1: Choose five different photos of yourself. What does each one reveal? Write your observations down and reread them over the next three days. This will become the basis of a brief, yet fair, autobiography that tells not only others, but you, too, who your better Self is.

_____

_____

_____

_____

_____

_____

This exercise can also accomplish something else. By closely observing YOU in several photos, you can gain a better perspective of how others perceive YOU.

Exercise 2: Do others see your better Self when they look carefully at photos of you? When they look at you face-to-face? How can you know for sure? Is it important for you that they do?

_____

_____

_____

_____

_____

Your better Self can be seen in any photo of your face. Practice examining different regions of your face as you look at photographs of yourself. Peer intensely with no pretense or fear. Peer until you begin to look like anybody else you've ever seen in your life. It will be at that moment that you see yourself as any other person worthy of your time and attention. This is the true you, different from the "you" you think you already know. This is the embodiment of your better Self.

Exercise 3: Look at your reflection in a mirror. Which "you" do you see: the "you" you want to see or the "you" you've always seen? Do you see it? Do you really see who you really are—and who you really can become? When you do, say hello to your better Self!

_____

_____

_____

_____

_____

_____

THE REAL YOU—IN REAL TIME

Facebook is one of the most popular social networking groups on the Internet nowadays. But is a Facebook friend a real friend? What is a real friend? Did people make friends before Facebook came along? Did they make real friends? Who are your real friends? Are they on Facebook?

> **Exercise 1**: Sit down. Get quiet. Think back on a recent experience you had with a stranger, someone you had never met before. Can you recall what went through your mind as you first saw this person? How did you feel about seeing this person? Were your thoughts more about how they might see you—and think of you—than about your curiosity about the kind of person they might be? If so, what did you think they thought of you at first glance? How much does it matter what they thought or what they think of you now?

> _____
> _____
> _____
> _____
> _____
> _____

Is Kenny Wallace, the NASCAR driver, real? Of course he is. How he sees himself will not be the same as how you see him, but his own personal "reality" is as real as he wants it to be to others. In other words, he has a choice regarding who he will be in his relationships with others—the Self he sees himself to be or the Self he thinks others want to see. You have the same choice.

In junior high school, I did a curious thing. One of my classmates was particularly accomplished in music. He was also smart—at least his grades indicated that he easily mastered the subject matter of all of his classes. I also heard some teachers talk about how gifted he was. A sense of inferiority engulfed my mind. I felt insufficient, inadequate, that I wasn't good enough or smart enough. I wanted to be better and smarter; I wanted to be like HIM.

Thinking that his abilities would somehow be instilled in me if I merely acted as he did, I began to imitate his every behavior. What he did, I did. I sought to acquire his inner aptitude by adopting his outward attitude.

It didn't work. All I succeeded in doing was to annoy him and make myself miserable when I finally learned that I wasn't any better for having "copied" him. I eventually learned that to become better at anything I wanted to do meant that I had to better understand and appreciate the real me, with all it's perceived greatness—and shortcomings.

The real YOU is the one who is free from the desire to be someone else. You not only have what it takes to become your better Self, you also are good enough, smart enough, talented enough to make it so. When you fully realize this, you'll hear your better Self say, "Thank you!"

Exercise 2: "To wish you were someone else is to waste the person you are." Do you agree? Do YOU wish you were someone else? Why?

_____

_____

_____

_____

_____

_____

Exercise 3: Who are your real friends? Are they their better Selves today? How can you help them become their better Selves, if they aren't already? What are they doing that is helping you become your better Self?

_____

_____

_____

_____

_____

_____

Exercise 4: What circumstances bring out the best in you? Write them down. What can you do to ensure that those circumstances occur more frequently than they do now?

_____

_____

_____

_____

_____

_____

BLESSED BY THE RIGHT PEOPLE

Negativity is like having a gun aimed at your head. You feel addled and paralyzed, suddenly stuck in a quagmire of procrastination. But when an affirmation appears, like a positive bolt out of the blue, if you've thought something nice about yourself, or if someone—it doesn't matter who—has tossed you a life raft in the form of a word of encouragement—it can make all the difference.

> **Exercise 1**: Who makes your life worth living? Who has helped you see your better Self more clearly? Who has saved your life by tossing you words of positive reinforcement? Who has pointed the pistol not at your head but into the air and pulled the trigger to start you on your way to becoming your better Self? Write down the names of those persons. Contact them and thank them. Do it today.

_____

_____

_____

_____

_____

_____

You've probably heard the story about the tortoise and the hare. The tortoise proceeds, never quitting, while the overconfident hare dallies too much, quitting and running in spurts—and eventually loses the race.

How did the tortoise motivate itself to win? I think the tortoise won because it was well aware of its capabilities—and its limitations—relative to those of the hare. It knew what it was up against and drew on its strengths of persistence and plodding determination to focus squarely on the goal to win. It did not allow anything about the hare to cloud its vision of the goal. Besides, the hare would do what it wanted to do in any event. As it turned out, the hare lacked self-discipline because it overestimated its own abilities and underestimated its opponent's. It thought it *would* win because, all things taken into consideration, it *should* win.

The hare could have easily won but it did not take the goal—or the race—seriously. Ironically, the hare lost because it thought it **should** win and the tortoise won because it thought it **could** win. Often, stories like this ancient tale of Aesop, encapsulate the essence of what it takes to live a successful and peaceful life. When you come across such literature, it is a blessing.

Words have power to create a reality in the heads and hearts of those who hear or read them. When that reality says that you have what it takes to be a winner at the end of your journey, then you WILL win regardless of the atmosphere (positive or negative) of any environment in which you find yourself along the way. Such blessings enable your better Self to emerge in all circumstances, even those that would strongly argue against your chances to win.

> **Exercise 2**: Who are the people whose words are blessing you at this time in your life? What are those words? Could you repeat them to yourself? What would happen if you did? Could you do it any time you wanted?
>
> This is how you can make the blessings you receive blessings for others: **_believe the blessings_** (accept that others can help you become your better Self by what they say to you), **_become the blessings_** (embody the spirit of the words by repeating them often to yourself) and **_bestow the blessings_** (pass them along to others by means of your stories—show them how their stories can be about their better Selves by telling the stories of how you became your better Self).
>
> What is the story your life is telling today? Is it the one you want told? How can you change it, if you wanted to?
>
> _____
> _____
> _____
> _____
> _____
> _____

We all have the right people in our lives who constantly bless us by their presence and their stories. They might not be alive anymore—but they are always *there*, at the tip of our minds, helping us become—and remain—our better Selves.

> **Exercise 3**: What specifically have others done to help you become your better Self? Could you do that for someone else? If you aren't doing this for others, why not?
>
> _____
> _____
> _____
> _____
> _____
> _____

WALK A MILE MORE

Don't judge anyone until you've walked a mile in their shoes. It's true. We tend to draw conclusions about people very quickly, with little introspection or retrospection—or appreciation for their unique journeys in life. When wrong conclusions are drawn, and action based on those erroneous conclusions is taken, harm is frequently done. The greatest harm is actually to ourselves because we close ourselves off from a valuable resource—the perspectives on life of others whom we have voluntarily cut off.

> **Exercise 1**: Have you been quick to judge someone you know? Have you decided to dislike or blame someone that you don't know except via second-hand or third party sources, like the news stations on TV or on the radio or in the newspapers? Is this behavior ever an example of your better Self?
>
> _____
> _____
> _____
> _____
> _____
> _____

It is even better to walk a mile in someone else's shoes, especially someone you don't like. At least while doing this with an open heart and mind, you gain another perspective. Unfortunately, rigid mindsets are the rule among human beings, not the exception. Refuse to remain imprisoned by a closed mind and heart. It is the height of arrogance and ignorance to assume that you cannot learn from those with whom you disagree or whom you perceive to be quite different from yourself.

> **Exercise 2**: Read a biography of a famous person that you DON'T admire. Try to read about this person's life without judging. Do it with an open mind. What have you learned that you didn't know before? Did anything challenge—or change—your initial perceptions of this person? Do you think you've become a better person for having done this exercise?
>
> _____
> _____
> _____
> _____
> _____
> _____

This person's journey, no matter how apparently different from your own, contains elements of YOUR better Self. Read with anticipation and expect to meet elements of yourself that have remained elusive precisely because you didn't think you could learn from someone who appeared to be so different from yourself.

Walking a mile in another's shoes means freedom from a narrow perspective. I once heard someone say that a rut is nothing more than a grave with the ends kicked out. What that means is that the mental, emotional and spiritual ruts we create and comfortably live in throughout our lives only serve to bury our better Selves and smother our worthy aspirations.

Don't let this happen to you . . . any longer! Expand your perspective to resuscitate your better Self.

DAILY DECISIONS

The foundation of your life, and if you look deeper, of your better Self, can be found not in great turning points of existence, but in little moments, a multitude of little moments. Our lives are cumulative—even as children.

It's good to make decisions, especially the small ones, in harmony with your values. But this doesn't always happen. Sometimes the "flow" of your decisions can begin to shift against your better Self. This occurs when you fail to conscientiously consider the consequences of your seemingly inconsequential decisions throughout the day. Every decision impacts others in some way, like the expanding ripples of the wave caused by a pebble tossed into a pond. Without considering this impact, our decision-making becomes rooted in selfishness.

Such decisions cumulatively compromise your conscience, spinning your moral compass erratically, dashing your better Self against the rocks of self-absorption and pride. After a while, you become unhappy and bad choices come to characterize your daily decisions.

Sensing the disconnection between your better Self and your decision-making, the growing ambivalence toward the results of your decisions causes you to become internally conflicted. Consequently, you lose motivation and commitment to achieving any of your goals or manifesting any of your worthy aspirations. You become convinced that you are NOT worthy of what you truly want.

> **Exercise 1**: STOP! Contemplate your next decision that you'll make today. Who will it affect? How will it affect them? Do you care? Should you care?
>
> _____
> _____
> _____
> _____
> _____
> _____

A conflicted individual is capable of committing the greatest evil because it becomes easier to overlook the negative impact and dire consequences of "simple" decisions. It also becomes easier to conflate evil with good—or to confuse the two, thinking that one is as "good" as the other. Those who do so may perceive themselves as noble or heroic performing great acts in the service of society, but they care little, if at all, about the consequences of what they do. After all, if evil is as good as the good, what does it matter the consequences of one's decisions?

When good is no longer distinguished from evil, evil reigns supreme because there is no standard against which to measure its perniciousness.

Having a clear distinction between good and evil results in unambiguous decisions designed to benefit the common good. When the distinction is muddled, the common good is rarely benefited but is often corrupted and harmed.

Decide how you will decide! Will you make your little daily decisions in the spirit of service to self without consideration of others? Will you make them in the spirit of helping others become their better Selves? If the former, you'll find your own better Self drifting further and further away. If the latter, you'll discover the true power your better Self possesses to make good things happen.

> **Exercise 2**: Write down the decisions you need to make today and how they will affect you and others. Think beyond the decisions and their immediate consequences. Who will be touched and in what ways? How will these long-term and long-range ramifications affect people's motivation and abilities to become their better Selves?

What I Will Do Today:	_All Potential Consequences:_
_____	_____
_____	_____
_____	_____
_____	_____
_____	_____
_____	_____
_____	_____

Exercise 3: *"If you chase two rabbits, both will escape."*

"In any moment of decision the best thing you can do is the right thing, the next best thing is the wrong thing, and the worst thing you can do is nothing."
—Theodore Roosevelt

"In the long run, men hit only what they aim at. Therefore, though they should fail immediately, they had better aim at something high."
—Henry David Thoreau

What do these quotes from well-known successful people mean to you?

Would you agree with Eleanor Roosevelt that, *"It takes as much energy to wish as it does to plan?"*

WHAT YOU'LL DO TODAY

Exercise 1: Think about what you're going to do today. Why are you doing these things? Do you really have to do them—today? Why not tomorrow? What will happen if you don't do them today . . . or even tomorrow?

_____
_____
_____
_____
_____
_____

Contemplate your actions. Consider your plan for today. For every moment you spend in such meaningful discussion with yourself, you gain three in productive results.

The key is FOCUS. Target your energies so that you know precisely what you want to do, and where to point your day. Mentally describe what the end of the day looks and feels like. It takes a little energy to do this, but it gives you back a great deal of energy, in the form of momentum.

Momentum toward your worthy aspirations always makes you feel good, strong, confident and in control. It also reduces stressful reactions throughout the day and creates the emotional environment in which peacefulness and wholeness can be consistently experienced.

Exercise 2: How are your worthy aspirations and your better Self related? Isn't this akin to the chicken and the egg conundrum? If your worthy aspirations are needed in order to elicit your better Self to manifest them, but your better Self is needed in order to clearly see your worthy aspirations, which comes first? Does it matter?

_____
_____
_____
_____
_____
_____

Write down what you'll do today:

1. _____

2. _____

3. _____

4. _____

5. _____

6. _____

7. _____

8. _____

Which of these arise from your worthy aspirations? Which of these activities will take you closer to your worthy aspirations? If any of them don't, reconsider their worthiness of your time and effort to do today. What else could you do instead that would be a better use of your time? Always remember that everything you do—and choose not to do—either moves you closer to or further away from your better Self.

LOOK BEYOND YOUR SELF

We all are like deep lakes, not shallow puddles. But most of the time it seems that most of us remain on the surface of our selves, content with shallow and simplistic interactions with others. By failing to look beyond our "surface selves," we can only see the superficial in others, as well. We pass judgments based on the face of things, choosing not to explore any further.

This is the lazy person's approach to living. It takes energy to go beyond the shallows of the self and the meager depths of ordinary experience. It also takes courage.

But how do you gain the courage to seek out what otherwise might remain unexplored? How can you overcome the innate human fears of learning who you really are—warts and all?
A good technique is to BE with yourself.

> **Exercise:** Write down three questions you have about the meaning and purpose of your life. Go to a room alone. Close the door. Sit in a chair, but not a recliner. Observe how you feel at this moment. Close your eyes. Pay attention to your breathing, your heartbeat, to any momentary discomfort or physical pain you are feeling. Ask yourself aloud the three questions you've prepared, one at a time. Give a full minute to each question. Try to listen without any words going through your mind.
>
> Do this for at least three full minutes. When you're finished, stand up. What did you just discover? Write it down immediately! What will you do with what you've discovered? How will you use it to help you arrive at your better Self?
>
> Is there more to you than meets others' eyes? Than meets your own eyes? If you think so, use this exercise to look beyond your self and beneath the surface to see your better Self.

_____

_____

_____

_____

_____

_____

"Energy flows where attention goes." When you pay attention, you learn. Your mind prepares itself to receive new information and to see things in different ways. Preparing meaningful and purposeful questions about the meaning and purpose of your life beforehand is a marvelous method to focus your attention on what matters most for you at the moment.

Whatever you're dealing with in your life can be boiled down to a single question or a series of questions. The difficulties you experience at any given moment are merely the result of unanswered questions about the meaning of your life and your purpose for living. Get clear on the questions so you can get clear on the answers by looking into the soul of your better Self.

Remember the Russian dolls: inside each of us is a tiny version of all of us. When you can see your own better Self, the better Selves of others present themselves to you in every interaction, bringing out the best in everyone.

RISING TO THE OCCASION

If an accident occurred, and your friend's life was in jeopardy, could you rise to the occasion to help save him/her? How likely do you think it would be that you would step up?

You can be assured that you not only can but WILL step up if you live every moment summoning your better Self by being *"better self-conscious."* At any time, especially in times of difficulty and challenging situations, call up the power of your better Self by simply stepping up to do what needs doing. Rarely is anything more needed than merely moving to take charge of the situation. This is also called "leadership." There is a leader inside you aching to take charge in circumstances that right now would cause you to faint because of fear and self-doubt.

Leadership is not just about making right decisions. Perhaps what is more important it's about making decisions right. What do I mean by that? Instead of fretting endlessly over the decisions that must be made, a true leader will make a decision based on available information and input from others and then work to make it the right decision. No matter what your situation at present, your better Self can always find effective ways to make it right.

Your better Self rises to *any* occasion . . . if you let it. Let it. Let it lead. You could wind up saving someone's life, or at least leading them to their better Self, which, for some, will be life saving.

Exercise 1: Whose life depends on you? Do you believe you could save someone's life if they needed your help to live? Perhaps they need your help to live their lives better than they are now. Could you help them live . . . better? How?

_____

_____

_____

_____

_____

_____

Exercise 2: Have you ever saved somebody's life? If you have, how did that make you feel? If you haven't, do you think you ever could if called upon to do so? Would you be scared?

_____

_____

_____

_____

_____

_____

OVERWHELMING CIRCUMSTANCES

Examine this precise moment of your life. Be alone with yourself as only you know how to be. Be honest. What are your circumstances like at this very moment? Are they good or bad? What makes you think 'good' or 'bad'?

Sometimes appearances really are deceiving. What starts out seeming to be bad, might end up really, really good. What begins seeming to be good, might end up really, really bad. Another aspect to consider is that what's good for YOU may not be good for anybody else. What's bad for you may not be bad for anybody else—or not quite so bad perhaps.

The point is that your life experiences change moment by moment. Sometimes these changes are subtle, and don't seem obvious when they are happening. It's like watching a tree grow. How can you discern its growth *as it is growing*? It is a process that occurs in its own time and at its own pace—and change is the means by which it happens. Your better Self fosters personal growth by patiently participating in the process and welcoming change when it becomes an option for improvement.

As they occur throughout the years, changes can take us from one perspective to another, sometimes conflicting perspective—and back again. If you become emotionally and psychologically attached to your current perspectives, you'll find it immensely difficult to contemplate the possible benefits of other perspectives or the need for changing anything about yourself. Your perspective on your current circumstances can become hardened causing them to become overwhelming.

When this happens, it's time to:

a) Retreat into the bathroom.
b) Pet the cat.
c) Pet the dog.
d) Pet the aardvark.
e) Read the Bible or other Holy Book
f) Count to ten—or a hundred!
g) SMILE!

I'm not going to tell you the answer. If you've been communing with your better Self, you'll just KNOW. Your answer at this time might not even be on the list above. (Have you ever actually seen an aardvark?) However, in time, your right answer will present itself. Wait for it . . . wait for it . . .

If you chose "g" as your answer, while smiling, revisit the circumstances that seemed so overwhelming just a moment ago. Are they so bad now? Seriously, did your smiling do ANYTHING at all to help you gain control over your circumstances? Did smiling help you shift your perspective on your circumstances, even just slightly? If it didn't, what else can you try to overwhelm them with a more positive perspective? Remember Shakespeare's admonition: "There is nothing either good or bad, but thinking makes it so."

Ask yourself, "What's good about my predicament? Am I missing anything about the facts of this situation? In what ways can I look at this differently? How can I turn it into an opportunity?"

Take a deep breath. Let it out. Don't hold it in. That's an ineffective way to try to control your surroundings. If you ever tried to manipulate your parents' behavior toward you by threatening to hold your breath "until you turned blue"—did that ever work? If you ever turned blue, it wasn't because you held your breath on purpose.

Will what seemed like overwhelming circumstances help you discover your better Self? Most of the time, adverse circumstances can help you like nothing else can. It is a most precious gift to be given the opportunity to change a negative into a positive, to shape something that starts out "bad" into something that proves to be good for many people. Your better Self gratefully receives such a gift and works hard to be worthy of it.

> **Exercise 1**: What about your attitudes have "hardened" to the point of inflexibility, perhaps even cynicism? At what point do you say, "Don't confuse me with the facts, my mind is made up?"

_____

_____

_____

_____

_____

_____

> **Exercise 2**: Where does your "hardness" show up in your relationships? Has anything good ever come from such hardness? What can you do to soften your perspectives to allow more flexibility in the ways you deal with the circumstances you face at any given moment?

_____

_____

_____

_____

_____

_____

Exercise 3: How have your perspectives on major themes in your life changed over the years? Why did they change? Was it for the better?

_____

_____

_____

_____

_____

_____

Exercise 4: When was the time you felt you grew the most as a person? What were the circumstances that caused your growth? Were they "good" or "bad?" How did you know at the time? What caused your circumstances to change, if they did: something from outside or inside yourself?

_____

_____

_____

_____

_____

_____

Exercise 5: Do you agree with Shakespeare's admonition: "There is nothing either good or bad, but thinking makes it so?" Why or why not?

_____

_____

_____

_____

_____

_____

WORKING WELL AND WORKING RIGHT ARE TWO DIFFERENT THINGS

A clock on the wall is functioning perfectly but it's keeping the wrong time. We've all experienced this phenomenon at least once, maybe as many as thirty-seven times in our lives. The clock is working well, but it's not working right.

Your life can be like that clock. Are you sailing along smoothly, but going in the wrong direction? A friend of mine hated to travel by airplane. He rushed from airport to airport, often frantic and frenzied. One day he boarded a flight, but didn't quite notice where the plane was heading. Safely in his seat, he was tired and fell asleep. Many hours later, he woke up in a pleasant mood. Seeing a flight attendant, he flagged her to his seat.

"Are we almost to Oakland?" he asked.

She regarded him strangely for a moment. He assumed it was him. He felt that people were always regarding him strangely.

Finally, she said, smiling, "Oakland? This plane is going to Auckland!"

The plane was working well, very well indeed. In fact, it was almost at its intended destination. But that didn't matter a whole lot. My friend ended up in New Zealand where he discovered his better Self on an unplanned but much-needed vacation. He never felt that people regarded him strangely again.

When he returned to the United States, he quit his high-level job that he had risen to through one promotion after another and began working as a flight attendant. It was his dream job. Even though he didn't receive nearly as much compensation for his work, he was happier because he knew he was "working right." Now he goes frequently to the place where he was introduced to his better Self and laughs all the way there and back marveling at his good fortune to be able to work well and work right at the same time.

> **Exercise 1**: Where are you working well but not right? What are you going to do to change that starting today?
>
> _____
>
> _____
>
> _____
>
> _____

_____
_____

Exercise 2: What is stopping you from pursuing one of your worthy aspirations that you haven't begun to work on yet? What can you do today that will help you take your first step toward manifesting it in your daily life? TAKE THAT STEP NOW!

_____
_____
_____
_____
_____
_____

THE PARABLE OF THE MAN, RICH

Reading about the man, Rich, a lesson that can be gleaned is that owning a multitude of material possessions is not necessarily everything it's cracked up to be. Such ownership, while potentially a blessing in the short term, isn't a sure bet to bring you closer to your better Self.

In fact, it more likely will be a source of obfuscation (look this word up), like a fog that obscures your view of a distant horizon. You see the fog bank and you know that there is something on the other side that you can't see. If the fog never lifts, eventually it becomes your reality and you lose your desire to venture through it to explore the reality beyond.

The man called Rich was a hoarder of possessions. He enshrouded himself in the fog of self-concern. Your better Self is not about possessions. It's about your personal assets, especially your character attributes and how to use them for the benefit and edification of others—when the time is right. When you apply your personal assets in this way, you truly become "Rich," even if your name is something else entirely.

Once a sage took his pupil to a window and asked, "What do you see?"

The pupil replied, "I see people coming and going."

The teacher then placed a mirror in the window. He asked his charge, "What do you see?"

The student said, "I see myself."

The master spoke in a whisper: "The window is glass and the mirror also is glass coated with silver; as soon as silver is added you no longer see others, but yourself alone."

Seeing only yourself is not always a bad thing, especially if you are engaging in introspection, self-examination and exploration of your better Self. But if, after reaching your better Self, you keep it to yourself and hoard it from others, you become like the man, Rich, without ever experiencing the wealth of your better Self.

> **Exercise:** Contemplate an occasion when you've been greedy. What was the outcome of your greed? Did you feel "richer" afterward? Did you feel good about yourself? Was your energy level up or down? Were you satisfied with your efforts? Did anybody else besides you benefit from your "greed?" If so, for how long? Was the outcome a manifestation of any of your worthy aspirations? Would you do it again? Why or why not? Don't let this exercise slide. Do it and you'll learn a lot about how to become your better Self.

MAKE THE LUNCH YOU REALLY WANT

The construction workers described in the story in the book didn't always like their sandwiches. But the most "tragic" case of an unwanted lunch was when the ham sandwich was actually made by one of the griping workers.

We all "make our own lunch," so to speak. This means to make decisions, and every decision has consequences.

> **Exercise 1:** Can we fully accept the consequences of our actions when we refuse to accept responsibility for them? It seems that many people want to accept the good consequences of their actions while refusing to accept the bad ones.
>
> What does accepting responsibility for your actions mean? Do you know anyone who only "takes credit" for the good consequences of a decision but refuses to "take blame" for bad ones? How do you feel toward them? When you accept responsibility for every consequence of your decisions, what might happen in your relationships with others? How would they feel toward you?

Excuses are easy to make. The meaning of an excuse is quite literally to "excuse yourself" for actions that you have already taken. Why should you be granted a reprieve every time you make a mistake? We don't like it when political leaders make excuses for inappropriate behaviors, "misspoken" words and poor judgments. Why won't they admit their mistakes, especially when such mistakes may prove harmful to their constituents or to the country and when, by admitting them, they could minimize any negative impact they might have?

Why won't they? They are human beings. But that's the oldest excuse in the book. "I'm only human!" is used so frequently as to be a caricature of humanity. A mistake, as Henry Ford observed, is the opportunity to being again more intelligently. In other words, a mistake is an opportunity to learn a better way forward. And the first step to learn from a mistake is to admit that it was not what you wanted to happen.

Unfortunately, those who make mistakes perpetuate and magnify their bad consequences by not taking complete responsibility for having committed them; when they don't, they cannot learn from them—or correct them—or make a more intelligent effort in the future.

World leaders and celebrities aren't the only ones who refuse to take full responsibility for their actions. They're just the most visible. Someone you know might also be guilty. Who is this person? He or she will stare back at you, perhaps in disbelief, when you look in the mirror.

> **Exercise 2**: Being guilty of making mistakes does not have to translate into feeling guilty about having made them. Raise yourself up to your tallest standing position, take a deep breath in and blow it out with a guttural sound and say aloud, "I have made a mistake; it is not the end of the world or the end of my life; I will learn from it and seek to not make it again; I will begin again more intelligently and with greater wisdom; I am worthy to learn from my mistakes and to become my better Self nevertheless."

_____
_____
_____
_____
_____
_____

What's for lunch today?

CONCENTRATE ON ATTITUDE

Our attitudes are as important to us as every part of our physical body. If your perspective on living is sour, if you've gotten into the habit of finding fault with everything around you, your better Self may become lost, or at the very least misplaced like one of your favorite socks—the ones that went so beautifully with your favorite suit.

But how do you know if your better Self has been lost? If it is, can you find it again?
You might be due for what I call an "attitude assessment."

Examining your attitude can be painful—like sticking yourself with a needle, only there's usually no blood lost. Let's begin. Brace yourself. Hold on to your seat.

Exercise 1: Ask yourself these probing questions: Am I more often negative about myself and others than positive? How does negativity manifest itself in my life? How do I feel when I'm being negative? Why do I feel this way? Is it difficult for me to turn a negative into a positive? Why?

_____

_____

_____

_____

_____

_____

Exercise 2: Identify five negativity triggers—habitual behaviors by you or others that invariably lead to negativity. Negativity is like a cancer—it can relentlessly influence and infect every single action you take, and these actions, in addition to enduring negative consequences, can eventually lead to depression—a case of the "blues" that won't go away. What can you do to make sure that these triggers are never pulled by you or others again?

_____

_____

_____

_____

_____

Now it's time to take positive action. You have identified some negative aspects of your current self. Can negative attitudes, especially those that have become habits, like a chronic illness (yes, your negative attitudes can manifest themselves as illnesses!), be transformed into something positive? In other words, how can you make lemonade out of lemons—especially when you wanted to drink orange juice?

Think AFFIRMATIONS. Tell yourself that you *can* do something, not just assume that you can't. Such positive self-talk is your best antidote to the poison of negativity.

But it's hard to talk nice to yourself when you're not grateful for being yourself. If you're not grateful for being YOU, it's probably because you're focusing more on your momentary circumstances than on your enduring ability to overwhelm them with the positive resources of your better Self.

Remember that you can always have an attitude of gratitude. Just concentrate on ways you can begin to manifest your worthy aspirations by being your better Self. Believe me when I say that, if you do this, you'll find all sorts of reasons to be grateful for being YOU.

Don't dwell on regrets. "Could haves," "should haves," and "what ifs" are the hobgoblins of ambivalent and conflicted minds. In essence, they're like the residue of attitudes that once existed, but that are now about to be forever changed by your better Self.

Negative attitudes can have long-term ramifications. Let's say that you fill a bottle with vinegar then rinse it out and put water in it. If there is even just the slightest residue of vinegar in the bottle, the entire volume of water will hint of the taste and odor of vinegar.

Such it is with negativity and regret. If your attitude is going to be positive and lead you toward your worthy aspirations, no hint of negativity or regret can be present in your mind. Concentrate on attitude—not just any attitude—but *positive* attitude.

In aviation, attitude is the measurement of your relationship to your surroundings, especially the ground; more specifically, it is the angle of an aircraft in relation to the direction of the airflow or to the horizontal plane. This means that if you are leaning in one direction, you are leaning away from the opposite direction. In other words, you can only be moving in one direction at a time.

This is true of your mental attitudes. You cannot be of two minds. Single-minded pursuit of your worthy aspirations means releasing all negativity and regret from the background—and the forefront—of your mind. It is erasing completely all negativity and regret and replacing them with positive expectation of living everyday as your better Self.

> **Exercise 3**: List any regrets you have been concentrating on recently. Why are you feeling regretful? What can you do to redeem your regrets? What can you choose to concentrate on instead of your regrets? How will that help you become your better Self?

PUT YOUR BEST ATTITUDE FORWARD

Before we go out to meet someone, especially for the first time, we might brush our teeth, apply deodorant, comb our hair, and apply other desired cosmetics, as our parents told us that "first impressions" are very important. All these preparations are essential, but even if we're "looking marvelous," we might have neglected the most important thing. When we meet a new person, almost immediately our *attitudes* come under scrutiny. If you don't put your best attitude forward, like your "best foot," you run the risk of ruining the impression you want to make.

You can force yourself to be cheerful, and smile, and this can be an excellent strategy, as our moods, either happy or miserable, are less dependent upon our circumstances than we might assume. Simply choosing to be in a better mood can improve your mood.

But sometimes it doesn't work, or comes across as contrived. If the underlying habit of a bad attitude is what's at your core, if your self is mired in negativity and deep down, you know it, then it's time to get acquainted with your better Self.

You can do it now. Here's how:

Go to the nearest mirror. Look into it. Who do you see? Someone who is more than you have become or someone who has become all you will ever be? When you answer this question, you will become acutely aware of what your true potential is.

The question you must ask yourself now is, *"What one action must I take immediately to begin tapping the resources I now believe I possess to become my better Self?"* Write your answer down here:

_____
_____
_____
_____
_____
_____

Now, do it. When you do, you unleash your better Self to help you manifest each of your worthy aspirations. Oh, happy day!

Exercise 1: Are you really grateful today for being you with all your potential as well as all your "baggage?" When you're truly grateful for being YOU, you've become your better Self and are on the path to achieving your worthy aspirations. Do you believe this? You can become more grateful for your life by doing something for someone else. What can you do today for someone else that will help them become their own better Self? Take that first step and plan to do it . . . now.

Exercise 2: Think of a time you felt you were "acting" to be the person you thought others wanted to see. How did you feel about not being "yourself?" Does your better Self ever need to "act" to be itself?

YOUR WORK IS NEVER DONE

It sometimes seems that we are buried alive amid a cache of unfinished work. My appointments, meetings, travel itineraries, projects, and "relationship work" with family and friends can seem like an infinite stream of challenges and opportunities. Ever wish for a vacation? I have. Occasionally, I even get to take one, but then, guess what? The moment I'm back there's more to do—an endless succession of a myriad of tasks to complete.

Sometimes I find myself ruminating on work that's waiting for me *while I'm still on vacation.* It's as if I can't be fully content at home thinking about work or at work thinking about home! Trying to live in both worlds simultaneously causes ambivalence, uncertainty, self-doubt and anxiety.

But all this prompts another question: do you live to work or work to live? We all must earn a livelihood unless we have unlimited financial resources. However, even those with wealth work at various passions. Work is an essential part of the fabric of being human—even if it's working to avoid work!

If we "live to work" we may be missing the boat. While the saying of being "married to your job" has a great deal of truth in it, if it really becomes "all there is" as far as you are concerned, then your chances of discovering a "better you" have just been drastically reduced.

Even though your work is never done, work doesn't have to define YOU. Work that flows from your better Self and that is in service of manifesting your worthy aspirations is pursued with passionate determination. This kind of "work from your heart" actually increases your physical energy and stokes the fire of motivation for ongoing accomplishment. It is the consummate expression of your better Self.

Any work you do should follow the model that children enjoy the most—"playing" to the exclusion of just about anything else. An eight-year-old child was asked by his mother, "What are you doing?" when he was observed stacking his mashed potatoes onto his plate and then digging into the potato mound he had created with a spoon.

"I'm exploring," he replied.

"You're also making a mess," the boy's mother told him. But to the boy, it wasn't a mess that he'd created.

"It's not a mess," he informed his mom, "It's Potatoland."

What are the chances that this boy, if he continues in his wonderment and creativity, will be able to merge his work and play into something new, bold and refreshing? If not squashed by the swamp of negativity that infects the general society, his better Self will emerge from his imagination. His work will arise from his play and be conducted in a playful manner.

Could you work like you're playing?

Exercise 1: Albert Einstein remarked, "Imagination is more important than knowledge." Was he right? Why or why not? If he's right, what does this mean for the way you work—and play?

_____

_____

_____

_____

_____

_____

Exercise 2: In what way does your work define who you are and who you see yourself to be? What would you be working at if you weren't doing what you're doing now? If you changed jobs, do you think you'd have more time for other things you enjoy doing more? Why do you work at the job you have now? What would you do if you didn't have work to do? Would you play all day long? Could that play actually be work, too? How does work help you become your better Self? Do you have to work to become your better Self?

_____

_____

_____

_____

_____

_____

Even though your work is never done, neither is your play when you are your better Self.

A final thought:

What's on your mind right now that has been "hanging fire," simmering on the back burner of your brain? Is there anything detracting from the fullness and enjoyment of your life and distracting you from your drive toward meaningful action to improve your life? This comprises the work you have yet to do to become your better Self. As long as what's "on your mind" remains in your mind, your work is never done.

Exercise 3: How could you "play" with what's on your mind today so you can "work it out?"

_____

_____

_____

_____

_____

_____

FENCE JUMPING

Backyards today are increasingly fenced in. Children growing up in suburban and residential neighborhoods don't necessarily have pastoral scenes on the other side of their fences, but temptations of various sorts still prevail in many areas—anything from fruit trees to sheds full of firecrackers might exist on the "other side." Some fences today are much higher than the ones I knew as a child—perhaps even eight feet high and crowned by spikes. These would undoubtedly be difficult to jump over.

Why would you want to jump over them anyway?

> **Exercise 1**: What are the fences you've built that are keeping you on this side of your better Self? Are they helping you live a peaceful life? Have you ever felt like you wanted to just jump over them or tear them down altogether? What made you feel that way? Did you do it? If you did, what did you find out about your "need" for the fences? What did you discover about the phrase, "the grass is greener on the other side of the fence?" Was it?

_____
_____
_____
_____
_____
_____

It might be dangerous to jump some fences without getting impaled. Instead of jumping over them, why not consider walking around them? It might take a little longer but it would reduce the chance of injury. Either way, there's something inside urging you to break out of the common environs you're used to living in.

> **Exercise 2**: When you're feeling "fenced in" start to think of the reasons why you feel that way. Is there something on the other side that is beckoning you to "come hither?" What might that be? Sometimes the grass IS greener on the other side of the fence. Have you become "comfortably miserable" in the garden you've been keeping and yearn to expand your yard?

_____

_____

_____

_____

Oftentimes, jumping fences is the preferred exercise of your better Self. What fences do you need to jump today?

THE CHOICE OF CHARACTER

Boundaries can sometimes be annoying for those free spirits among us, but we all need *some* limits. A little structure goes a long way in guiding your daily decision-making, and channeling your inherent attributes on your way to your better Self.

Without boundaries, lacking limits or structure, your effectiveness as a person can meander like a blind beast foraging for sustenance while straying further and further from its home. Freedom is best understood as that which allows us to choose our own boundaries rather than that which allows us to be uninhibited by them.

When you are free to choose whatever you want, you must be acutely aware of what will work and what will not work. In other words, your freedom to do whatever you want **_includes_** the freedom NOT to do whatever you want, especially if it will harm others. What governs all subsequent choices is your initial primary choice of character. You must first choose your character because character influences every choice you make.

If you want to make choices rooted in your better Self whose consequences move you deeper into your better Self, you will need to choose a character of *self-discipline*.

Self-discipline involves being willing and able to defer personal gratification. In a society of instant gratification, where anything you want can be obtained almost at the moment the desire for it arises, delaying gratification is a difficult notion to entertain. If you can get it when you want it, why would you want to wait to have it until later . . . if ever? The logic seems alien.

Have you ever purchased something you really wanted and found that it wasn't what you expected? Even if it was, how long did it take for the "new" to wear off? Getting what you want when you want is often unfulfilling. It can also leave you with a feeling of emptiness and an attitude of "is that all there is?"

Character has been defined as what you do when you know no one is looking or who you are in the dark when you think no one can see. This is only a partial definition. Character is also what you do in the midst of other people and why you do what you do.

You can't hide the true nature of your character for very long. You cannot perform for an extended period of time beyond the level of your true character. The old cliché is correct: "The truth will out." Examples abound in ancient literature and throughout history as well as in contemporary society of people being brought low by "unintentional" slips of the tongue or by exhibiting behavior that is blatantly hypocritical from their stated beliefs and carefully polished persona.

Character is fashioned out of how we choose to deal with our experiences in life. It's not the experiences themselves but how we interpret their significance for our lives and how we allow them to inform the way we treat others. The root of character is self-discipline. The boundaries you impose on yourself regarding the ways you think and act form the disciplined heart of your character.

A more complete definition of character is that it is the manifestation of your inner energy of thought and attitudes as these are either harnessed and directed with purpose or uncontrolled and allowed to flow in multiple directions without intentionality. In the former situation, this energy becomes focused and powerful, like the mighty Niagara River being effectively channeled by its banks toward the great Falls, there to be displayed in beauty, grace and immensely beneficial strength.

In the case of the latter situation of this inner energy not being given effective boundaries, it rapidly dissipates in strength as it becomes increasingly diffused of focus and errant in direction. In fact, such unfocused energy actually contributes to destructiveness. It is ironic that the devastating power of floods is actually the result of the weakness of the boundaries imposed to channel the waters toward constructive ends.

Our behavior is either goal achieving or tension relieving. By that I mean that our lives are either guided by consciously established goals or they are controlled by instinctual urges. When we set goals, we're simultaneously setting parameters for our thinking and boundaries for our behavior. These are the only tools we have that will help us accomplish our goals: our thoughts and our actions. They must be consciously directed toward a destination in order to help get us there.

Self-discipline is choosing what you will allow yourself to be bounded by; it is setting the solid banks within which your inner wealth will be securely contained. By setting goals, you are taking an active role in shaping and directing the inner energy of your mind and the results it will create.

Thought and behavior can then be seen to be either "on task" or "off task" regarding what results they produce. If the result is that a goal is achieved or that you're moved closer to its achievement, then the behavior is "on task" and, therefore, "goal achieving."

On the other hand, we all are familiar with the anxiety that often accompanies concentrated effort and the occasional feelings of being overwhelmed by the task at hand such that we retreat into behavior that momentarily relieves that tension. But this behavior takes us off task and results in goals not being achieved or moved closer toward. Such behavior can actually move us further away from any goals we have set.

James Allen, in his book, "As a Man Thinketh," said it well when he penned, "For you will realize the vision of your heart, be it base or beautiful. You will fall, remain or rise with your thoughts . . . For you will become as small as your controlling desire or as great as your dominant aspiration."

High quality character consciously chooses to persistently pursue "on task" thinking and behavior that helps to manifest the noble aspirations of self-improvement and selfless service of others while refusing to be drawn "off task" by the multiple trivial desires we all possess that seek to take control of our thoughts and actions. This sort of character is high quality because it has first set its direction by willingly choosing beneficial boundaries within which its energy can freely and swiftly flow toward advantageous objectives.

Those desires that try to control us are all based in selfishness and seek to satisfy the natural human drive to place Self above everything else. Once we give into them, it becomes easier to give into them again because the immediate consequences of having done so don't appear to be so bad. We didn't die, no one was hurt and we still feel we're in control of making our dreams come true.

Eventually, however, after many times submitting to them in preference to "on task" action that would have moved us closer to achieving our goals (dominant aspirations), they become the dominant influence in our decision making. They define by default our existence. They're the first things we think about and the first things we do when the pressures of trying to accomplish a worthy aspiration confront us, as they inevitably will.

Our lives eventually demonstrate the effects of continually giving in to these petty desires: we begin to believe we can no longer make our dreams come true or achieve great things for ourselves and others. We become paralyzed by a lack of self-confidence to do anything that will help us become better than we are now.

It takes concentration and dedication to achieve worthwhile goals; it requires the ability to "power through" the moments when the controlling desires insist on whispering loudly in our ears, "you don't need to do this; this is way too difficult; you can get by with less effort; this is not necessary in order to get what you want; this is not what you need to be doing right now; you should be doing something fun and enjoyable; take a break and seek some pleasure in your life . . ."

The 'concentration-breakers' can be endless. What are yours?

I'm not saying that it's wrong to take breaks from important tasks. In fact, by not taking them regularly you're actually siphoning off the energy and focus you have to give them. You grow tired physically and emotionally indifferent. The longer you stay "on task" the more power you give to the urges to get "off task." This is a matter of pacing your pursuit with purpose, not chasing your goal relentlessly regardless the consequences.

It is important to understand that the things you do that you don't have to will always determine who you are and what you'll be able to do when it's too late to do anything about it. This applies equally to your discipline of achieving goals and fleshing out dominant aspirations as well as to acceding to the siren songs of trifling desires. What you do in this regard traces the dimensions and plumbs the depths of your personality. This is the crux of character as well as the crucible in which it is formed.

Who you are and what you're able to do in any given situation—your character—results more from what you do that you don't have to do than from those actions which are expected of you. Recall the partial definition mentioned earlier: "character is what you do when you know no one is looking or who you are in the dark when you think no one can see."

The things you do in the dark or when no one is looking are those things that you really don't have to do. But you do them anyway because high quality character not only goes the "extra mile" but goes the "invisible mile," as well.

If you are free to do anything within the Law and Reason that you want, then an intrinsic part of that freedom of choice is the freedom **not** to do what you're otherwise free to do. This is self-discipline by means of imposing boundaries on our personal freedom that purposefully limit the range of choices we set for ourselves.

These choices will be centered on goal achievement and "on task" thinking and behavior. Consequently, they direct activity within the mind and the body that may involve doing what "doesn't need to be done" in order to accomplish goals or to enlist others in helping you do so. These "needless" actions can be described as the salt of a high quality character that is focused more on others than on the Self.

High quality character is not constrained by a simple utilitarian engagement with the world or by a pragmatic approach toward relationships. There is more to life than merely getting what you want out of it.

The quality of character you possess depends on the boundaries you choose within which you make all other choices. These boundaries, then, depending on their integrity of strength, provide the channel of your power and significance in the world. You will become as great as your dominant aspirations if you choose to route your thoughts and behavior within the boundaries of goal achievement or as small as the controlling desires that take you off task and diminish the value you place on your Self and what you can accomplish with your life.

I have unfettered freedom to do whatever I want tomorrow. But how can I structure my day so that at the end of it I have accomplished—or am well on my way to accomplishing—what I have chosen to achieve?

> **Exercise 1**: Following is a goal setting process that will work every time you use it. All you need to do is follow the examples below replacing them with your own goal statements, and then determining if they are direct or indirect time boundaries. A direct time boundary is one that specifies specific times in a day for the task to be done; an indirect time boundary is one that refers to an activity in a day that can occur at any time but that must be completed by the end of the day.
>
> > I will get up early in the morning (6:00) and go to bed at a moderate hour in the evening (10:00), thereby receiving an ample amount of regenerative sleep. (Direct Time Boundary)
> >
> > I will eat the proper kinds of food at mealtimes to avoid indigestion or stomach complaints and to receive the proper nutrition my body needs to feel well and perform optimally (Indirect Time Boundary)

I will read for at least one hour as my "mind food." (Indirect Time Boundary)

I will work for exactly four hours on my special projects (8:00 am to Noon). (Direct Time Boundary)

_____
_____
_____
_____
_____
_____

As outlined and with your details filled in, your goals will help you define not only the boundaries of your impending day, but will clearly reflect your primal choice of character.

Exercise 2: It can also be very worthwhile to set loftier goals with a higher or even transcendent purpose in mind. If you practice incorporating goals that manifest self-improvement or selfless service into the framework of your day, your "day" can evolve into a "mission." A mission is "an aim or task that somebody believes it is his or her duty to carry out or to which he or she attaches special importance and devotes special care" (Encarta World English Dictionary). Do you believe your daily tasks can be "duties" with special importance to which you devote special care? Approaching your daily activities with such an attitude will inevitably result in satisfying accomplishments that have long-term positive ramifications.

_____
_____
_____
_____
_____
_____

Exercise 3: Another of Ralph Waldo Emerson's wise quotes is: "People do not seem to realize that their opinion of the world is also a confession of character." How are you "confessing" your character today? Does it reflect "positivity" or negativity?

_____
_____
_____
_____
_____
_____

Exercise 4: Albert Einstein observed, "Weakness of attitude becomes weakness of character." What does a "weak" attitude look like to you? Do you agree with Einstein that attitude and character are intimately linked?

_____

_____

_____

_____

_____

_____

Exercise 5: What are your "controlling desires" that take you "off task" from accomplishing your goals?

_____

_____

_____

_____

_____

_____

Exercise 6: "The true test of character is not how much we know how to do, but how we behave when we don't know what to do."—John W. Holt, Jr.

The foundation of character is not so much "right" knowledge as it is a "right" attitude toward the knowledge you have. How do you act when you become aware that what you know is either not correct or not enough? How do you behave when you know you don't know what you need to know to make good decisions?

We can't know everything. How we behave in the midst of ambiguity and "gray areas" is not only the true test of our character but also the experience we need to judge the quality of our character. Do you have high quality character? How do you know for sure?

_____

_____

_____

_____

_____

_____

Exercise 7: "It is important to understand that the things you do that you don't have to will always determine who you are and what you'll be able to do when it's too late to do anything about it." What is your take on this? Is it ever too late to change your character, even if you change your mind and your behavior? Can you actually change your behavior without affecting your character?

_____
_____
_____
_____
_____
_____

Exercise 8: What goals have you set for yourself that you're having trouble achieving? Why do you think you're having trouble? Could it be because you haven't set clear boundaries within which to make good decisions about what to do to move you closer to your goal? What boundaries should you set today that will help you channel your energy toward satisfactory achievement? What would stop you from setting these boundaries?

_____
_____
_____
_____
_____
_____

Exercise 9: "No horse gets anywhere until he is harnessed. No steam or gas ever drives anything until it is confined. No Niagara is ever turned into light and power until it is tunneled. No life ever grows great until it is focused, dedicated, disciplined."—Harry Emerson Fosdick

What does this mean for you today?

_____
_____
_____
_____
_____
_____

Goal setting can soon have you walking toward your better self—at a quickened pace.

The Principle of Healthy Desire

Goal setting can be difficult when it's difficult to prioritize our desires. Which goals are worth setting? Which goals are important? Which goals are inconsequential—especially when you take the long view? Answers to these questions depend on how you see your goals helping you realize your desires to manifest your worthy aspirations.

There are healthy desires and unhealthy desires. An unhealthy desire is one that distracts you from your worthy aspirations while a healthy desire moves you steadily in their direction.

Healthy desire keeps your eyes on the prize of your better Self by working to turn your worthy aspirations into reality. You have a unique voice, still and small, that speaks inwardly telling you the best ways to go for your goals. When you listen for it you'll hear it expressed most clearly and strongly in the yearnings of your heart. In other words, your inner voice, unique to YOU, speaks through your healthy desires urging you to make your worthy aspirations real. If you listen long enough—and often enough—you'll hear precise directions for how to do it, too.

> **Exercise 1**: Your unique voice is also your inner muse. What is it telling you to do now, at this very moment? Can you hear it or do you need some sort of "instrument" to amplify its sound? What might such an "instrument" be?

_____

_____

_____

_____

_____

_____

Besides relatives and people you have known who might once have filled your mind with misguided advice, there are those OTHER VOICES. These can act like detours within your mind. They are distractions and time-wasters—preaching procrastination and "you can always do that someday" as their chief message.

These indirect voices—diversions like mind-numbing television programs, movies, and endless surfing on the Internet—are really thieves relentlessly robbing you of your most precious gifts: your desire to realize your goals and aspirations and the time you need to do so. Such distractions cause conflict and inhibit your evolution toward the culmination of your aspirations.

Your worst enemy, when it comes to realizing your aspirations, is AMBIVALENCE. Ambivalence results from halfhearted desire—or "divided" desire. This kind of desire is always unhealthy because it leads to feelings of uncertainty and hesitation that can quickly cloud your vision of your future and swiftly erode your passion to pursue your worthy aspirations. Such feelings can turn your first tentative steps toward your aspirations into a sad parody of your dreams.

Unhealthy desires create inner discord and discontinuity that leads you to pursue unhealthy practices and meaningless goals.

Both healthy and unhealthy desires create habits of doing and **not** doing. Remember **stay, stop, start** to help you identify what you're doing that's actually working, what you're doing that's not working and what you need to do to alter these so you can become more effective at achieving your goals.

Exercies 2: What do you need to *stop* doing today that will help you achieve a goal? What do you need to *start* doing? What do you need to *continue* doing to a greater or lesser degree? Answering these questions will give you extreme clarity on your next steps toward your better Self.

_____

_____

_____

_____

_____

_____

Exercise 3: What is distracting you from your worthy aspirations today? How can you get your focus back on what really matters to you?

_____

_____

_____

_____

_____

Your better Self is the object of your healthy desire. All other desires are distractions.

The Art of Listening

Listening is truly an art. To do it well, you might as well be painting or sculpting or writing, because the same amount of concentration is required. You don't even need acute hearing to listen, although it helps. Theoretically, a deaf person can listen intently to their own heartbeat, or to the trilling of a bird, or to their best friend's chatter, and they can do it without hearing a peep. The art form is all about concentration.

When we don't concentrate on another person, we aren't really listening. Half-listening or casual listening can be coy, but it seldom leads to real communication. A good listener is a person who concentrates well. They tend to maintain good eye contact.

While engaged in listening, the LISTENER sits attentively, except for the occasional "rebooting" I mention in the book. The idea is to be as patient and relaxed as possible.

You might also ask questions to indicate that you are indeed interested in what the other person is saying. Your questions should be courteous while tapping your own wellspring of wonder—never facetious or mocking, or in any sense condescending. Silly queries can't be ruled out entirely, if your purpose for asking them is to elicit and provoke further discussion by means of temporary levity. In fact, if a silly question is armed with a purpose, it's never really silly at all.

If you fancy yourself to be an interesting person, you might become an excellent listener. But you'll never become the listener that you can become if you don't genuinely *enjoy* listening and practice your newfound skill in the manner of an art. A large part of the art of listening is being authentically *interested* in the speaker.

Always show your gratitude to the speaker for the amazing bounty of wisdom and experience that they are providing. Speakers love feedback, and listening is a form of love. Make your listening an intentional practicing of your art. Let it become bold and fresh and unafraid—just like your better Self.

Have you ever thought that you might not be a good listener? Even if the thought never occurred to you, the following signs are good indicators that you might need to consider learning to listen better. If you do, you'll discover that you'll get a lot more accomplished with less stress and rework while enjoying your work and life much more.

Here are some strong signs of poor listening skills:

➤ You receive large amounts of written communication

> You receive the same information repeatedly from the same people

> You are infrequently delegated complicated tasks

> You spend a lot of time putting out fires (reactive behaviors take up most of your work time)

> You learn about important information and events late, or not at all

> You notice that people talk a lot to each other but not to you

> You find yourself doing the same things others have already done

If you're experiencing any, or a combination of these signs, don't fret. You can learn effective proactive listening skills easily and quickly. There are a number of resources available on the web and through your local education institutions. All it takes is your willingness and desire to improve your communication efforts toward both understanding others and being understood by them.

However, even with the best of skills, there are circumstances under which communication, especially listening, can be a challenge to achieve. Here are some of them:

> Lack of concentration - you find it difficult to stay focused on what is being said and your mind often wanders

> Emotional deafness - you really don't care enough about the other person to want to listen to what he/she is saying

> Physical distractions - ambient noises and movements in the immediate environment

> Boredom and disinterest in the subject matter being discussed

> Self-importance - you've "heard it all before" or you think you know what the other person is going to say before they say it

Here are seven ways to begin to learn better listening behaviors. Keep in mind that the more you employ these behaviors the sooner they'll become healthy habits that will aid in effective communication every time it is attempted.

Seven Steps to Listening Well

> Use empathy - ask yourself, "what is this person teaching me?" and "how is this person reminding me of my own experience?"

> Suspend judgment - don't draw any conclusions until you've heard everything that is said

➢ Tolerate silence—the meaning of the message lies often between the spoken words

➢ Listen for total meaning—understanding is circular in that the whole can only be grasped in terms of its parts, but the parts can really only be fully understood after the whole has been completely divulged; mentally confirm the meaning of the message both as it is being sent and after it has been sent

➢ Ask questions—this gives evidence of your involvement in the process of communication as well as provides the means to ensure that you're "getting it right"

➢ Take notes—if this is appropriate, this activity can make sure you understand as the message is being conveyed

➢ Slow your thinking rate—you can think a lot faster than anybody can talk; slow your thinking rate to match and mirror the speaker's rate of speech so that you can get into the flow of thinking of the speaker—this will put you both into the same psychological and emotional rhythm and make empathetic listening easier to do

Exercise 1: Which of these seven steps to listening well will you choose to begin improving immediately? What will you do to improve—starting today? How will you know that you've improved?

_____

_____

_____

_____

_____

_____

M. Scott Peck, in "*The Road Less Traveled,*" wrote eloquently of the potential union that can occur between a speaker and a listener when certain practices are adopted:

"An essential part of true listening is the discipline of bracketing, the temporary giving up or setting aside of one's own prejudices, frames of reference and desires so as to experience as far as possible the speaker's world from the inside, step in inside his or her shoes. This unification of speaker and listener is actually an extension and enlargement of ourselves, and new knowledge is always gained from this. Moreover, since true listening involves bracketing, a setting aside of the self, it also temporarily involves a total acceptance of the other. Sensing this acceptance, the speaker will feel less and less vulnerable and more and more inclined to open up the inner recesses of his or her mind to the listener. As this happens, speaker and listener begin to appreciate each other more and more, and the duet dance of love is begun again."

Exercise 2: Ask someone to listen to a story you want to tell. Observe the ways they listen. Now, ask them to tell you a story or relate an experience they have recently had. After they have finished, ask them to rate you as a listener. On a scale of 1 to 10, with 10 being the best, how would they rate your listening behavior? How do they rate their feeling of being listened to? Of being fully understood? Ask them for at least three specific behaviors you exhibited that made them feel that you really understood what they were saying.

If you are rated less than "8" you should seriously consider practicing the techniques and using the tools contained in both the book and this self-study manual. Even if you're a "10" you will notice immediate improvement in your confidence as a listener as well as the positive responsiveness of those you're listening to. You'll both feel better about YOU.

_____
_____
_____
_____
_____
_____

Exercise 3: What are the challenges you face when listening to someone? How do you overcome them? Do you try? Why or why not? Do you really believe that listening is a good quality to have? Do you really think it's necessary in order to have good relationships with others?

_____
_____
_____
_____
_____
_____

Exercise 4: Do you believe you can "bracket" yourself while listening to another? What will you do to bracket your feelings in a tense conversation?

_____
_____
_____
_____
_____
_____

Effective listening is the art of your better Self. It invites others to experience the art of their own souls and to express it in a "dance of love" accompanied by the music of their better Selves.

THE SET OF YOUR SOUL

We've all witnessed people positioned in meditative poses, and such images convey a sense of peace. Harmony must certainly exist within that person, we reckon. If this happens to be true, then that harmonious spirit becomes the seedbed out of which their better Self grows. Peacefulness produces the power you require to manifest your worthy aspirations.

Peace is the absence of conflict—but it is something more. It's the psychological, emotional and spiritual environment that fosters development of our inner resources—like courage, passion and determination—and enables us to use them whenever we need them. In the absence of internal peacefulness your external reality is always characterized by ambivalence, doubt and hesitation to some degree. This, then, takes your concentration off of what is worthy of your desires and efforts and diverts it to less important, more easily completed mundane "jobs." These jobs, however, usually don't move you closer to your worthy aspirations, rather, away from them.

We sometimes greet each other with such phrases as, "How are you doing?" The 'prescribed' response is typically something like, "I'm doing fine," even if we're not. But do we really care to listen to any answers we might receive? Do we actually expect anyone to care to listen to our answer? Under these circumstances, not to care in the sense of really wanting to listen, is not problematic because these casual social interactions and customary greetings are meant to acknowledge others while politely communicating the desire not to enter into further conversation. We can't talk in depth to everyone we acknowledge, even if we really wanted to.

Next time you're greeted in such a routine manner, try responding a bit differently. Instead of reacting with how you're *feeling*, respond with your assessment of your *state of being*. Are you at peace? Are you in control of your mental, emotional and spiritual environment? If you are, your reply might simply be, "I'm peaceful," or "I'm whole." How about, "I feel like petting my cat?" What reaction might such an answer to a "care-less" question elicit? Try it and find out.

As a magnificent cool spring morning caressed the beautiful tree-studded campus of Drew University, one of my professors and I crossed paths—literally. With neither of us breaking stride, I exclaimed, "How about this gorgeous day?"

His reply? He inhaled deeply and, as we passed each other, he sighed loudly. Your better Self sighs in response to the beauty it experiences every day, expressing an appreciation and gratitude for living that goes beyond words.

What in your life is beyond words to express? Could it be that it is beyond words merely because you have never tried to put it into words before? Try to do that now. Don't worry if you can't; only worry if you've never tried.

Exercise 1: What single word would you use to describe the state ("set") of your soul right now? Is this word truly adequate to describe your state? Do you find that you need more than a single word? No matter what words—or how many—you use, is this description the one you really want ascribed to the set of your soul? If not, how will you change it?

_____

_____

_____

_____

_____

_____

Exercise 2: What is your definition of inner harmony? What does such a state look and feel like to you and to others? How do you know? Can you feel peaceful even if you're in pain?

_____

_____

_____

_____

_____

_____

Exercise 3: How do you get inner peace if you don't possess it now? If you're not experiencing peacefulness, what one thing will you do to invite it into your life today? Can you become peaceful merely by "acting" peaceful?

_____

_____

_____

_____

_____

_____

HAPPY CAMPER

My story about Scott reveals a lot about an extraordinary man, and also about how resilient we can be. Resiliency is a wonderful aspect of your better Self. Scott's aspiration of speaking to Zig Ziglar was realized because it was worthy of him. Your aspirations can assume a special significance during times of adversity.

I came into Scott's life at the right moment to be able to bring him and Zig together for their mutual benefit. It was more than coincidence that I had developed a relationship with Zig just prior to meeting Scott. In retrospection (and introspection), it is clear to me that my connection with Ziglar was established more to benefit Scott than me. And that is as it should have been. It contributed to making Scott—and continues to help me be—a happy camper.

You have no doubt heard the expression, "Every cloud has a silver lining." Is that really true? Not if you don't intentionally look for it. When dark clouds gather and threaten to obscure your view of your better Self, remind yourself that these clouds have linings that will only give up their "silver" when diligently searched for.

> **Exercise 1**: The Roman philosopher and poet, Horace, said, "Adversity reveals genius, prosperity conceals it." Do you believe you have genius within you that can only be called forth under difficult circumstances? How would you describe your genius?

What aspiration, if achieved, no matter what you've endured, or perhaps *because* you've endured difficulties to achieve it, would make you a happy camper?

> **Exercise 2**: List five times in your life when you discovered a "silver lining" in the midst of trouble. In what ways can these help you better understand what you're going through right now? Did these silver linings help you more clearly see—and be—your better Self even in the middle of the darkness of the outer clouds?

_____
_____
_____
_____

Exercise 3: Has there ever been a time when you were able to pass along the good things that happened to you to others? Did it ever seem that those good things happened to you just so you could pass them along to others?

_____
_____
_____
_____
_____
_____

Scott loved life and enjoyed it to the hilt even in the midst of constant and immense pain. He was peaceful in life even though he knew he would soon die. Do you know people who love to complain about life—even about the smallest of irritations—and how difficult their lives are? When it comes to thinking about "life after death," the question is not, "Does it exist?" rather, "If you don't enjoy and appreciate the opportunity to experience life as you know it, why would you want to extend your experience of it after it's over?"

Scott lives on because he chose to live as a happy camper even though the storms of life rained heavily on his tent.

OUR BELOVED SHADOW

"Who knows what evil lurks in the hearts of men? The Shadow knows." Between 1930 and 1954, Walter B. Gibson's famous radio character, perhaps the most famous of all time, kept Americans glued to their radios. A variation was later used during *Rowan & Martin's Laugh In*, a 1960s era TV show, and made famous by comedian Flip Wilson, as he voiced, "The devil made me do it."

Although cloaked in religious overtones and used to deflect personal responsibility, the latter also refers to our "shadow selves." The great psychologist Carl Jung realized that if we lose touch with those darker aspects of ourselves, keeping our "evil" thoughts, desires, and unworthy aspirations submerged within our unconscious, we do so at our own peril.

In other words, we are all quite capable of committing evil acts, whether we realize it or not. Instead of holding our "shadows" at arm's length, we should embrace them as integral parts of ourselves—not to commit evil—but to be aware of what "lurks in our hearts" so that we don't.

Repressing your shadow is not a good idea. The potential for adverse consequences is too great.

Exercise 1: Can you share out loud with anybody close to you some of the "evils" that you've committed? That most probably would be a dangerous thing to do. To do so might very well cause further "evil" to occur. However, the real test in managing your "shadow self" is in being honest with yourself about those deeds that you have done whose negative consequences, even if no longer evident, have caused disquiet in your soul. The first step to making peace within yourself (a primary trait of your better Self) is to be honest with yourself about where and when you've cast your "shadow" on others.

The second step to making peace not just within yourself but also within your relationships is to make amends. Whose forgiveness will you ask for today? Once you've identified this person/these persons, write out what you will say. Then contact them to set up a face-to-face meeting. This can be done over the phone; however, there is nothing like looking a person in the eyes when making an apology. You know immediately if it was accepted and if forgiveness was granted. You know without doubt that the shadow that had been engulfing you and your relationship has been chased away by the light of reconciliation.

_____

_____

_____

_____

_____

_____

When you don't come to terms with the shadow within yourself, hypocrisy and self-righteousness ensue. This leads to increasing cloudiness with fewer silver linings. How would you like to experience severe thunderstorms 24/7 with a forecast of more of the same indefinitely? It would be difficult to endure for long. But this is what we experience in our lives—and what others experience of us—whenever we don't successfully integrate the good and the evil within us.

If we despise our shadows, we also despise ourselves. Acknowledging your "shadow self"—perhaps more than any other single action—can help you perform the work needed to become your better Self, because your better Self comprises a balance between your good and evil inner aspects.

> **Exercise 2**: Read the following article I wrote a number of years ago. In what ways do its themes describe your own story of struggle to balance your inner drives toward good and evil? What single thought will help you become more balanced today?
>
> As you read, take notes to help you narrow your thinking about how you can become more integrated, balanced and whole in your daily life.
>
> As insights occur to you, capture them by writing them down. This will be not only therapeutic but also liberating. The freedom you'll experience from no longer bearing the unnecessary burden of feeling unworthy of your aspirations because of an intuitive sense of being "bad" will catapult you toward more successful living.

_____

_____

_____

_____

_____

_____

"Doing the Impossible: Balancing Good and Evil"

Early in my youth I became fascinated by the prospect of actually doing what science said was impossible to do. I learned from both the empirical and theoretical versions of mathematics that there are an infinite number of points between any point A and any point B no matter how long or short the actual distance between the two. A proof of this is the hypothetical experiment that if I stand any distance from a wall and go only half the distance to it with each step, I should never actually get to the wall.

Mathematically, this experiment is possible to conduct; physically, it cannot be done. However, we are all in the habit of "touching walls" without any thought about how to do it or expending any effort in accomplishing this familiar feat.

I can actually touch the wall at any time I choose no matter what distance I am from it when I begin my approach toward it. The math says I cannot traverse infinity because infinity has no beginning or ending. However, the distance I cover between myself (A) and the wall (B), comprising an infinite number of points, indicates that what is finite can include what is infinite and that the infinite can be experienced within the finite.

In other words, the two concepts, as commonly assumed, are not mutually exclusive. Each exists only in relationship to and as an integral part of the other.

Life is a Balancing Act

The human being, just as a coin, can only exist at the nexus of opposites. Heads and tails comprise the coin and not merely one or the other. The one cannot exist without the other. Everything physical as well as metaphysical is manifested and experienced as a combination in equal degree of opposing forces.

On the cellular level, for example, atoms are composed of a central nucleus surrounded by electrons and positrons, which are elementary particles that have the same mass but opposite electrical charges. These particles counterbalance each other and identify the atom as a specific entity distinct from all other matter. Gravity, no matter how scientifically explained, is nothing more than the unseen force that pulls against that which pulls against it. The magnetic force is simply the equilibrium between positive and negative poles that are aligned exactly opposite each other.

"Who Knows What Evil Lurks in the Hearts of Men?"

The primary set of opposites that forms the human soul is good and evil. This dialectic describes the essence of human existence. Evil without the counterbalancing good causes the soul to be ill formed resulting in narcissism and destructive behavior toward one's self and others.

You cannot live in reverse, which is exactly what evil is—a drive toward death that seeks to reverse the natural impetus toward life. Interestingly enough, the English language just happens to provide what I think is an ideal illustration of the true definition of evil: 'evil' is 'live' spelled backward. And perhaps the ultimate description of "devil" is that he once "lived" but now exists devoid of any life.

This is the definition of evil I find most meaningful when dealing with human nature. Evil arises from the universal human propensity toward selfishness. It is the cause of all war and disharmony throughout human history. It focuses on self-preservation at the expense of others.

When your internal balance tilts toward evil, you begin to set yourself up as a god with dominion over everything in your universe. The lives of other creatures, especially other human beings, become insignificant and meaningless except as they play a role in serving to preserve your life and add to your personal increase. The resulting attitude and behavior toward creation sets the stage for conflict, struggle and revolt.

It is one of the mysterious ironies of humanity that when you focus exclusively on the preservation of your own life you actually wind up behaving in ways that gradually and imperceptibly destroy what you think you're protecting. Evil seeks to distract and eventually defeat the drive toward increasing life for all living things now and in the future by posing as intense interest in the defense of a single life.

Evil is manifested as much in a malevolent attitude toward life as it is in any wicked transgression or overt malfeasance. For example, do you know people who complain often about the circumstances and events in their lives, who feel constantly put upon by hardships, both real and imagined? They see their lives being manipulated by nefarious forces determined to make them miserable by thwarting their every dream and effort to improve their lives.

Mark Twain's comment, "I've experienced a great many calamities in my life; most of them never happened," applies to these people in that they make their lives unduly difficult because that's what they expect life to be. It is something to be trudged through, struggled against and tediously endured with stoic resignation. When these people die, they're glad it's all over.

This attitude is a manifestation of evil because it is antithetical to life. Evil only sees dearth and not abundance. It seeks death, not life.

In the "Happy Camper" chapter, I described how Scott had chosen life in the face of death. No matter how you slice it, this is not an easy choice to make. In fact, I think it is quite difficult because it requires a person to deny his or her natural predilection to cast blame rather than grasp responsibility. Even though you would be justified in calling Scott's fate a manifestation of evil, he was able to overcome it by means of his attitude toward it.

Although he would have been a wonderful father and wanted desperately to have a child he and his wife decided not to have children because they didn't want to take the chance of passing on his death gene to yet another generation. It was a courageous act of self-denial. I never heard Scott complain about the pain or the apparent injustice of his situation. In fact, he would frequently say with a big grin, "I'm a happy camper!"

Scott loved life and he wanted more of it than he knew he was to have. Nevertheless, he lived in joy and gratefulness and balanced the evil of his circumstances with the goodness of his attitude. I believe this attitude toward life prepared him to receive more of it after he died.

The Good Isn't Any Better

Conversely, good without the tempering of its opposite results in a soul that Abraham Lincoln whimsically described: "It has been my experience that folks who have no vices have very few virtues." Of course, vices and virtues are relative terms and I don't think Lincoln was speaking of anything other than human idiosyncrasies and certainly not of unmitigated evil.

However, without a definitive respect for the evil that comprises part of one's self, life becomes insipid, dull, disheartened, despairing, passionless and stunted in its significance. There's a healthy tension between good and evil that creates and sustains the human soul that, if pulled out of the nexus even slightly in either direction, causes deformation of character, distorted thinking and aberrant behavior.

You might think that it would be best for humanity and the world if the good within us were to completely overcome the evil within us. Ironically, when evil is omitted from the human equation life can actually manifest the evil it seeks to overcome or deny. Those who are horrified by the darkness they sense within them often will take great pains to exclude it from their consciousness thereby hoping to eradicate its existence altogether. Seeking to deal with evil by simply pretending that it doesn't exist actually creates the very circumstances out of which the dark side can better and more easily emerge into the world through our own actions.

Doug Hall, in his intriguing book, "The Reality of the Gospel and the Unreality of the Church," identifies the circumstances that could give rise to further evil in the world. He sees that human societies subconsciously seek to repress "the other side of the coin" of human existence. By means of their entertainment, social structures, media and often their religions they create alternate worlds in which there is only good, right, purity, brightness and nobility.

He cites an advertisement found in the New York Times several decades ago inviting people to the "unreal" world of Disney World in Orlando, Florida. It is written as if a father were writing to a relative or friends back home in the "real" world.

"One of the biggest, events of the day was about to happen. A parade. Leading the procession were Mickey and Minnie Mouse, followed by several marching bands and dozens of other famous Disney characters . . .

"Our children sat in amazement as President Lincoln got out of his chair. There before us was President Lincoln, as big as Life, speaking of the things that make countries great. As he sat down again, the star-filled sky behind him began to turn red. White clouds gathered and stretched across in bands, leaving a patch of blue at the upper left portion of the sky . . .

"After the Hall of Presidents, the children wanted to see Fort Wilderness where we got another glimpse of our great heritage. We met and talked with a man there whose name was Del Rosengrant. A real blacksmith . . .

"We left civilization for a while after that and traveled on four famous rivers of the world. The captain of our jungle boat safely guided us past hungry hippos, trumpeting elephants and spear-clutching headhunters. The kids really got a kick out of it and laughed aloud as my wife and I ducked from one of the elephants that threatened to squirt water at us.

"Everyone who worked at Walt Disney World always seemed to be having as much fun as the visitors. And of course the grown-ups were all having as much fun as the children. Walt Disney World was the kind of vacation our family will never forget. There was so much to see and experience. Together.

"And then comes the punch line, printed in bold capital letters so it won't be missed by all the anxious people:

'HOW YOUR CHILDREN SEE THE WORLD DEPENDS ON WHAT YOU SHOW THEM.'"

Hall offers his interpretation of the contrast between the sanitized "clean" world of Disney and the polluted "dirty" world of real life filled with fear and filth and, at the same time, with gallant self-sacrifice and inspiring morality. He understands well that the means to deal effectively with the dichotomy at the heart of life are learned or not learned in childhood.

"I remembered that I had shown my children Buchenwald. I also remembered that as we sat outside the Ploetzensee Memorial in Berlin, while I told my young son about the courageous people who had been hanged there for resisting the Nazis, he began to cry and accused me: 'Daddy, you tell me the most terrible things!'

"There are terrible things, and there will be. And when a people determines to protect itself and its children from them, it is quite probable that that people will become the cause of terrible things."

We are fooling ourselves when we believe we are doing good by sanitizing or ignoring altogether the evil within us. It is as difficult to do as minting a coin with only one side or imagining a stick with only one end.

Every summer I would attend church camp at Little Grassy Lake in southern Illinois. It was a glorious time spent in magnificent surroundings. One of the highlights of the week was playing "Keep Away" with a small beach ball in the swimming area of the lake. When I got the ball, if the opportunity arose, I'd try to finesse the opposing team by "hiding" the beach ball by tucking it under the water and sitting on it. But I was quickly found out because the pressure of the ball caused my body to gyrate wildly as I attempted to maintain my balance.

The ball was demanding to be seen. The further beneath the surface of the water I tried to stuff it, the more upward pressure it would exert.

Such it is with the things we try to hide from ourselves, the things we don't want to deal with, the frightening, the dark side—the other side of the coin.

Fyodor Dostoyevsky's, **Notes From The Underground**, contains some significant observations about the nature of the interior world humans carry within them. He writes, *"Every man has reminiscences which he would not tell to everyone but only to his friends. He has other matters in his mind which he would not reveal even to his friends, but only to himself, and that in secret. But there are other things which a man is afraid to tell even to himself, and every decent man has a number of such things stored away in his mind."*

This is What We're Made Of

So this is what we're made of: good and evil, however they are defined. In order to be fully human and alive, our task is not to run away from the dark side or to help our good overcome our evil. Rather, we are to keep them in balance, just as each atom exists only by the perfect pairing of the negative and positive particles that surround it. The well-lived and effective life of significance is the one that maintains and appreciates the natural balance between good and evil without allowing one to gain prominence over the other for very long.

There are events, initiated by others or ourselves, that will cause us to be so repulsed by evil that we seek to destroy any vestiges of it we sense within ourselves and others. There are also events that seem to compel us, as the once good boy Darth Vader of the Star Wars film saga would say, to "turn to the dark side," giving in to the path of least resistance by giving up our self-discipline to maintain perceived personal balance. The call to each soul is to persevere and persistently attempt to restore the balance between good and evil whenever it is skewed by the events in our lives or the poor choices we make.

"Do Not Give Up"

I was walking beside a beautiful stream recently in Independence, Missouri when I spotted these words that had been spray painted on a bridge abutment: "Do Not Give Up." I thought it interesting that such sentiment would be written in a place usually crammed with juvenile expressions of love and lament and the menacing phrases and characters from gangs of anti-social youths. I'm sure it was meant to encourage walkers and runners along the path to continue in their efforts to improve their health and endurance. But it also reminded me that this motto is exactly what we all need to live by every day in all our activities and undertakings.

Do not give up when it appears that it would be easier to do so. Do not give up when it seems that everything and everybody around you is strongly suggesting or even threatening you to do so. Do not give up in the face of seemingly insurmountable or "impossible" obstacles. Do not give up trying to balance your life even when something happens that lures you into thinking you've banished completely the evil within you or that moves you to want to simply give in to it.

What Does A Balanced Soul Look Like?

We've seen the disruptions and distortions that can occur in life when the balance is disturbed—in either direction. What happens when your soul is in balance? You experience what psychologists call "flow," where everything falls into the proper place, both mentally and physically. You experience creative energy and clarity of thought and direction that results in innovation and joy. Anything "new" stemming from human initiative arises out of remaining faithful to and faithfully in the tension between good and evil. This tension is truly the crucible of creativity.

I am not saying that you can only experience "flow" and creativity when you are in balance. I am saying that "flow" and innovation more often result whenever you have brought your good and evil into balance. You've no doubt heard that there is a strong connection between madness and artistry. I'm sure this can be true for external, visible art forms and expressions.

However, the inner artistry of the soul, out of which a flowing peacefulness, newness and joy are experienced, originates in the quiet balance between its opposing components.

Take Nothing For Granted

How do you create and sustain the balance? You take nothing for granted. You ask yourself every time you make a decision, "what will be the consequences for my internal balance and the lives of others who will be affected by this decision?"

Every choice you make has consequences for everyone involved. Will the choices you make result in you and others becoming self-righteous, bitter, angry, fearful, arrogant, unapproachable, resentful, condescending, lethargic or vengeful? Will they help you and others become enthusiastic, confident, courageous, bold, accepting, forgiving, self-giving, loving? Examining both the intended and unintended consequences of our choices—both before and after making them—is the perpetual task of self-balancing.

Lest you think that this is all too much of a chore to do consistently and successfully please know that we do this all the time anyway without being aware of it. In order for this subconscious activity to be of any value as a tool to help us maintain our personal balance, we need to raise it to conscious awareness so that we can begin to take more control of its effects in our lives and in the lives of others.

We create the quality and legacy of our lives by the choices we make every day. These choices are shaped by what we consider to be possible and impossible. Can good and evil in your life ever be balanced in the "impossible" way I've described or must they forever war against each other? Is it impossible to live a full, joyful, peaceful and productive life within the tension between good and evil? If you think it *is* impossible, then the only possible alternative is to be caught up in the battle between the two such that you experience life as a chaotic cycle of ups and downs, highs and lows, with only sporadic spells of serenity.

I call your attention to a statement that Jesus of Nazareth made when talking about how to treat those who do you evil. After saying that it is easy for anybody to love his/her neighbor, he proclaims that you should actually "love your enemy and pray for those who persecute you, so that you may be like your Father in heaven, since he causes the sun to rise on the evil and the good, and sends rain on the righteous and the unrighteous." (Matthew 5:43-45). This is tantamount to saying that you should do what you thought was impossible. If you think something is impossible, you won't try to do it.

Jesus was challenging his hearers to rethink what was possible for them to do. He knew that people experience good and evil on a personal and not an abstract level. His challenge was not that we should be exactly as God is, but rather to look at the good within us as originating from God and as the only proper response to evil. When this occurs, evil is counterbalanced with good and the resulting reality is one of peace, harmony and "flow."

Abraham Lincoln summed it up well when he asked, "Am I not destroying my enemies when I make friends of them?" Impossible? It depends on what you think. As Henry Ford said, "if you think you can or you can't, you're right!"

Exercise 3: Study van Gogh's *"The Starry Night"* below. What "themes" do you see in his setting? What is the overall meaning you get from it? What does it say about your better Self? About your worthy aspirations? What is that "black flame" to the left? Why do you think van Gogh put it there? Was it a mistake?

Imagine that the "black flame" divides the picture into two parts. What is to the right of it in the picture? What is to the left? Is there anything you can learn about your better Self by looking at *"The Starry Night"* in this way?

YOUR TRUE SELF-PORTRAIT

My son didn't want to ruin the picture, so he feigned happiness and glee. Even at the tender age of seven, he knew about his own self image, and about what he was projecting to others, even if he couldn't quite articulate it in words, and wanted to make his contrasting "self-portraits" somehow agree. But the stress of performing this "inner juggling act" brought him to tears.

Deep down, you have an idealized image of "happy you," the way you imagine that things are supposed to be, and ruining that picture can create a kind of cognitive dissonance—a kind of disconnect inside your psyche—that if it doesn't bring you to childlike tears—may well fill your heart with profound sadness. But if you become a "people pleaser" so as not to ruin an idealized picture that may not be true—you're asking for real trouble. To do this as a child is bad enough, but as an adult, it's infinitely worse because we become increasingly complicated in our perceptions as we move past life's stations.

> **Exercise 1**: Go get your favorite photograph of yourself. Gaze at it for a few minutes and answer these questions: 1) Why is this my favorite photo of me? 2) What was I doing and thinking at the time this was taken? 3) Could I have been merely "posing," trying to portray an image of myself that I thought was "better" and more pleasing to others than the way I was really feeling about myself? If so, why did I do that?

> _____
> _____
> _____
> _____
> _____
> _____

When we delude ourselves, we distance ourselves from any semblance of our better Selves. Self-delusion originates in the desire to portray yourself in an idealized fashion, and this only serves to obscure your view of the true YOU, your true self-portrait—your better Self.

> **Exercise 2**: Paste the photograph of yourself below that you think best depicts your better Self. Why do you think it does?

SELF-REINVENTION

Sometimes we arrive at places in our lives when self-reinvention is in order. This is the act of self-consciously re-forming our self-image to enable us to accomplish different aims than we have heretofore achieved or to expand our range of thoughts and behaviors in order to do something we've never attempted before.

> **Exercise 1**: List some adverse circumstances in your life when you needed to re-invent yourself. For instance, when you lost your job, when someone you loved died, or when your car broke down and there was no one around to help and you didn't have a cell phone with you. How did your thoughts about yourself change—or did they change at all? Did you immediately seek to alter your behaviors or did you merely continue to do the same things as a means of dealing with the issue? What happened if you did change? What happened if you didn't?

_____

_____

_____

_____

_____

Choosing to reinvent yourself always takes courage (which is the opposite of conformity). Self-reinvention, by definition, means that you are intentionally becoming a different person than the one others have come to know. This change will be challenging for both you and them. Part of the challenge will be their protestation of your attempts to change yourself. Do not let them talk you out of becoming a more complete, whole human being.

Often, the goal of self-reinvention is to become a better person, a better you. Often it is an attempt to escape from a version of yourself that you've grown tired of or that no longer provides satisfaction or self-fulfillment. Sometimes you must try something different if you are to achieve the goals you set because the "old" ways aren't working.

Reinventing yourself when you are challenged to go beyond what you think you're capable of doing requires that you tap into your inner resources. These internal assets comprise the enormous energy that is contained within you just beneath the surface of your conscious knowing.

By consciously reinventing yourself, you are knowingly probing the "hidden" places inside you seeking to access the creative energy normally not available. This energy exists only as the integration of opposites: much like the "north" and "south" poles of the magnetic field attract each other into harmonious union. Interestingly, poles of the same type repel each other.

On the surface, it appears that life is characterized by a battle between good and evil. This battle only serves to deplete our energy, squandering it on outcomes that always come up short in providing what we really want to experience. The battle, always being waged and seemingly never won, results in restlessness and lack of peacefulness. We feel "out of sync" with ourselves.

Self-reinvention enlists the energy of your better Self by purposely integrating the normally thought-to-be separate powers of good and evil. When this is done, you become more complete and effective as a human being. You become your better Self.

To cite Carl Jung, we're seeking *wholeness*. But our models for taking such re-inventive action are often incomplete and inadequate. As children, we are rarely, if ever, told or taught to become whole; instead the aspiration planted in our infantile minds involves "goodness," a conforming set of behaviors imposed on us from without that may have little or nothing to do with "wholeness." You may have been told to be a "good student" or a "good person."

As we approached adulthood, our initial partners may even have extended this inherently faulty concept to define a healthy and intimate relationship. Instead of two individuals coming together to find wholeness in themselves by means of their relationship with each other, relationships are too often thought to be good or bad based upon the "goodness," or lack thereof, of each of the partners.

> **Exercise 2**: Being good at something isn't necessarily desirable. For instance, the Nazis were good at executing large numbers of vulnerable people. What do you consider yourself good at doing that isn't really helping you become your better Self? Is it important to you that you continue doing something that isn't helping you become your better Self? If you gave it up, what else could you be doing that would be more worthy of your time and effort?

> _____
> _____
> _____
> _____
> _____
> _____

If we are to transcend ambiguity and conformity, and strive toward a sense of wholeness as opposed to "goodness," we absolutely must develop a knack for reinventing ourselves. Being whole involves striving to incorporate every aspect of yourself into something better, employing your inner resources in pursuing and manifesting each of your worthy aspirations.

Self-reinvention is the act of self-integration. The "reinvented you" draws its energy and sustenance from your better Self, which maintains a healthy balance between inherently opposing forces.

Your better Self is not a "good" self as opposed to a "bad" self. It is meant to be whole, which means to be balanced, integrating the good and the bad into a unique expression of wholeness.

> **Exercise: 3:** In what ways are you expressing your wholeness in your relationships today? In what ways do your relationships help to make you whole? How are you dealing with the inner tension that exists within you between good and evil? Do you believe you can harness the energy that is released when your inner forces of opposition are integrated into a balanced whole? Have you successfully integrated these forces? If so, how? If not, what do you think you need to do to start the process of integration?

_____

_____

_____

_____

_____

_____

FLOWING INTO YOUR BETTER SELF

Exercise 1: Concentrate on your heartbeat. Is your heart beating? If it's not you've got either a big problem or a big chance to make history. Lose yourself in the moment. The only thing that matters is—your heartbeat. This is the source of your life-flow and the primordial model for being "in flow." Notice that you don't have to do anything for your heart to beat, although what you do—and think—does have an impact on how well and how fast (or slow) it beats. What can you do to slow your heartbeat down today? If you slowed your heart rate, would this be a good thing? What might be some of the benefits?

_____

_____

_____

_____

_____

_____

Flow can be epitomized in other ways. Pro athletes often speak of being "in the zone" when they pitch a "no-hitter" baseball game, or throw a touchdown pass of fifty yards or more in football, or bowl a perfect "300" game.

A butcher I know, when making that ideal lamb chop cut, says that he knows when the cut is perfect, because he's "in the meat." I know when I've crafted the "perfect" sentence because when I read it over several times, it appears as if to have been written by someone else, and I'm reading it for the very first time. The words converge to express exactly what I want to say. Something within me "took over" and composed the sentence and the "outer me" learned from the "inner me." In flow, I become my own best teacher of how to live as my better Self.

There is a common thread with all these and similar scenarios. Flow occurs when what you want to achieve completely imbues your consciousness and dictates and directs the means for achieving it. The actions engaged to accomplish your objective occur seemingly of their own volition. You are flowing towards the larger reality of your better Self. Flow is most easily experienced when your worthy aspirations are the goals you seek to achieve. As your aspirations become real your better Self becomes more real.

But how do you get into flow? You must practice and develop "flow-worthiness." Here's how.

1. Challenging yourself is a crucial beginning. You must decide what you want to flow towards. It should be something that is not easily accomplished.

2. Don't procrastinate. Begin the process. Begin now.

3. Clarify exactly what you wish to flow towards. Set up a schedule, and an itinerary—as if you were about to take a trip.

4. Become your goal. Merge with it—like your heartbeat. Your goal and you are one.

5. Be confident. You are in complete control. Know this!

6. Discover each potential obstacle you can imagine and confront them, one by one, planning for any contingency. Reinvigorate your confidence as you "practice" flowing.

7. Visualize a positive outcome. Make the image vivid in your mind's eye.

8. Do it! Do it now! Go with your flow!

Exercise 2: Take fifteen minutes right now to go through these steps to begin to experience flowing into your better Self. This will be one of the most difficult activities you will ever undertake. Don't be afraid.

_____
_____
_____
_____
_____
_____

PART OF THE WHOLE

In the Book of Genesis in the Bible, the concept of "an original sin" arises. This is the sin of human vanity, where a person substitutes him/her SELF for God.

Most people don't think so esoterically, or at least not very often. For most contemporary human beings, becoming self-absorbed simply means becoming preoccupied and obsessed with trivial matters of SELF, being shortsighted and selfish in a greedy or vain way, and losing sight of our better Selves in the arrogance of self-centeredness. When this happens, the experience of wholeness, and of course, experiencing your better Self, can prove elusive.

Exercise: 1 What would you consider to be your "original" sin? Is this sin preventing you from becoming whole? If so, what can you do to make it right with those against whom you have "sinned" (including yourself)?

_____

_____

_____

_____

_____

_____

Exercise 2: In what ways are you helping your family become whole? Your community? The organizations you're a part of? In a profound, yet mysterious way, without your better Self they can never completely be part of the Whole. Do you agree?

_____

_____

_____

_____

_____

_____

You can only ever observe a part of the whole. When you look at a picture or a movie, what you see is only a slice of the context that surrounds your point of view. It's the same with any experience in your life. You cannot engage anything other than what is presented to you. However, you can become aware that there is something more than meets the eye. When you do, what is seen takes on wider dimension and deeper meaning.

By knowing that whatever you see is only a part of a greater whole you can adopt the attitude that there is always the possibility of expanding your current understanding of any situation to include more than what you can see. Every experience takes on a greater scale of significance that can result in surprising and unconventional perspectives. Knowing that there is more to learn provides motivation to learn more about what you already know—or think you know.

It's true that things aren't always as they appear. It's also true that everything, without exception, is *more* than what it first appears to be. What parts are you missing in your assessment of your current circumstances that might help you see that you are, indeed, a part of the whole that comprises your better Self?

_____

_____

_____

_____

_____

_____

_____

YOUR PURPOSE ON PURPOSE

Exercise 1: What makes you stressful? Why? What can you do about it? Will you do something about it? If not, what are you getting out of it to remain stressed?

_____

_____

_____

_____

_____

_____

You were born to manifest your worthy aspirations which, by doing so, results in you becoming your better Self. This is your purpose in life. You should not accept anything less, as to do so is to remain incomplete—not to mention unfulfilled. To lose sight of this truth, even for a moment, is to lose sight of your better Self.

To be purposeful in your thinking and acting in pursuing your worthy aspirations, you should consider what obstacles stand in your way. A consequence of your biggest obstacle, your concern about what others think of you, is stress.

When you believe that things aren't going your way, that others aren't thinking of you the way you want them to, anxious feelings can arise that threaten to subvert your resolve to pursue your purpose on purpose. You become too easily distracted and consumed by trying to control other people's perceptions of you—or even your own perception of yourself.

Stress results when you are out of sync with your purpose to become your better Self. It results from focusing on the obstacles to achievement rather than on the aspirations you want to achieve. Besides anxiousness and becoming easily distracted, other effects of being out of touch with your better Self include:

1) Personality change with the onset of depression combined with a sense of hopelessness

2) Feeling tense and increasingly irritable which results in volatile behavior

3) Acting on impulse without thinking about the consequences of your actions

4) Fears and phobias set in making it difficult to take actions that are rewarding or pleasurable

There are many causes of stress and many negative consequences. Whatever they may be, the following ***Stress Symptoms Checklist*** will help you understand how you are personally affected by stress. The goals sheets at the end of this exercise will help you think more clearly about what you can do to more effectively manage those reactions and turn them into more positive responses.

Complete this checklist to get clear on the extent of the stress you're experiencing presently. What parts of your life are being affected most adversely by stress? Why? What can you do to reverse the effects of stress in each part of your life? Who will you get to help you?

_____

_____

_____

_____

_____

_____

_____

Next to each statement answer either yes or no.

Physical Symptoms:

_____ Frequent Headaches

_____ Loss of Energy

_____ Digestive Problems

_____ Difficulty Sleeping or Insomnia

_____ High or Low Blood Pressure

_____ Loss of Appetite or Weight

_____ Heart Palpitations or Increased Heart Rate

_____ Rashes or Skin Problems

_____ Neck or Back Pain Spasms

_____ Decreased Enjoyment of Sex

_____ Chronic Fatigue

_____ Accident Prone

_____ Tight Jaw or Teeth Grinding

_____ Chest Pain

_____ Difficulty Breathing

_____ Poor Body Posture

_____ Increase in Perspiration

_____ Increased Frequency of Colds or Infections

_____ Night Sweats

_____ Dizzy Spells

_____ Difficulty Falling Asleep

_____ Change in Facial Expression

_____ Recurrent Physical Problems

Emotional Symptoms:

_____ Increased Irritability

_____ Isolating from Others

_____ Difficulty Concentrating

_____ Forgetfulness

_____ Increased Boredom

_____ Difficulty Making Decisions

_____ Tendency to be Annoyed by Little Things

_____ Shy or Overly Sensitive

_____ Constant Feelings of Dissatisfaction

_____ Hopeless Outlook

_____ Feeling like a 'Pressure Cooker'

_____ Depression

_____ Frequent Loss of Temper

_____ Over-Reacting to Situations

_____ Loss of Sense of Humor

_____ Feeling Nervous

_____ Difficulty Expressing Emotions

_____ Angered Easily

_____ Lack of Response to Emotional Situations

_____ Unknown Fears

Behavioral Symptoms:

_____ Unable to Relax

_____ Nervous Habits, i.e., Finger or Toe Tapping

_____ Trembling Hands

_____ Nightmares

_____ Compulsive Eating

_____ Nail-Biting

_____ Repetitive Thoughts

_____ Hair Pulling

_____ Loss of Interest in Appearance

_____ Trouble Getting Going

_____ Increased Smoking

_____ Nonstop Talking

_____ Work Absenteeism or Lateness

_____ Change in Use of Alcohol

_____ Procrastination

_____ Decreased Productivity

_____ Increased Drug Use

_____ Lack of Any Regular Schedule

_____ Bringing a lot of Work Home

_____ Workaholism

Now that you have a clearer understanding of how you react to stress (which, by the way, is another way of saying "lack of peacefulness"), fill out the ***Three-Step Stress Management Goal Setting Proces*** worksheets that follow.

The goal of this exercise is for you to determine:

      (1) What are your primary stressor sources?
      (2) What are the negative effects of the stress you encounter?
      (3) How do you think you should handle your primary stressor sources?

Three-Step Stress Management Goal Setting Process:

1. Primary Stressors (what triggers your stress reaction?):

_____
_____
_____
_____
_____
_____
_____

2. Negative symptoms of your Primary Stressors (ask yourself, "Why do I put up with this?"):

_____
_____
_____
_____
_____
_____
_____

3. Beginning today, how will you respond to your Primary Stressors? What will you do that is different from what you have been doing?

_____
_____
_____
_____
_____
_____
_____

When you are not purposely pursuing your purpose in life and tying it into your efforts to manifest your worthy aspirations, you experience stress. When you experience stress, you are not experiencing peacefulness. Which do you mostly want to experience throughout your life? Which one do you think is more conducive to calling forth your better Self?

Exercise 2: What are you "settling" for that falls short of your worthy aspirations? How do you feel about the compromises you've made? Why have you made them? Know that they stem from your greatest obstacle to becoming your better Self—that is, your concern with what others think of you. What can you do to stop compromising your better Self?

_____
_____
_____
_____
_____
_____

Exercise 3: What happens in your life that makes you feel "out of sync" with your surroundings? In other words, when do you feel like you don't fit in with "normal" reality? Why do you think you react this way under those circumstances? Is there anything you can do about it? If so, what?

_____
_____
_____
_____
_____
_____

TELLING YOUR TRUTH

Exercise 1: When was the last time you lied? Why did you lie? Was it a "big" lie or a "little" one? How do you know which it was? What were the consequences of your lie? Were they positive or negative? How do you feel about lying? How did you feel when YOU lied? How did you feel when you were lied to? Is lying always a bad thing to do?

_____

_____

_____

_____

_____

_____

We are sometimes lied to, and we sometimes lie. We deny that we do this, but we still do it. There are many kinds of lies, but why do we lie at all? It may be because we are afraid to tell the truth. The most frightening variety of truth is personal truth—YOUR TRUTH. Why does it frighten us so to reveal our innermost truths to another? Because we are sensitive to the opinions of others, we are afraid, and often intimidated by what we perceive to be another person's wholeness. In the glaring light of self-revelation, honesty can seem to be dangerous to our wellbeing.

One of the primary reasons we don't disclose of ourselves to others is the fear that, by doing so, we'll dispose of ourselves. Among the first words of the American psychologist Carl Rogers' book, "On Becoming a Person," are: _The most private is the most general._ In other words, what we hold back from others—and even ourselves—others are doing, too.

We all keep "private" those embarrassing moments, those "unacceptable" deeds and "shameful" thoughts, those humiliating failures and dreadful transgressions against others. As a result, they remain "out of sight" but not out of mind; in fact, being out of sight, they very often become the source of driving us out of our minds.

You cannot discover that you are isolating yourself from others, as they are from you, until you disclose yourself to them (not everyone, of course, but those whom you have come to trust and love). When you do, often you'll hear, "What!? You, too!? I thought I was the only one who felt that way (or who had an experience like that)!"

Keep in mind that we are all in life together and none of us has all the answers. So, ask your questions and help others ask theirs, because they will be similar—and the best and most satisfying answers will come when you tell each other the truth about yourselves.

Exercise 2: In what ways do you "self-disclose?" In what ways do you "self-disguise?" Why do you do either? When do you do either? Do you think that when you disguise your true thoughts and feelings about something you are "lying?" Is disclosing of yourself always telling the truth as you see it?

_____
_____
_____
_____
_____
_____

Exercise 3: What is the truth about YOU? Write your own obituary. Does it say only what you want others to say about you when you're gone or is it the truth about you? After all, your obituary is the final description of you that most people will ever read about you. If others knew your truth, would that be so bad? How could it be good?

_____
_____
_____
_____
_____
_____

You should be able to confront and examine your inner truths privately. You should be able to at least acknowledge them to yourself. Doing this—every once in a while—will supply the emotional octane for you to realize that despite your perceived unattractiveness—warts and all—*AND MAYBE EVEN BECAUSE OF IT*—you are still able to be your better Self!

But you can only be free to become your better Self when you face the truth of your tendency to practice self-deception about who you really are. You are more than you have become. And this truth about you will help you become your better Self.

Exercise 4: Are you keeping any secrets from yourself? If so, why would you do such a thing? What would happen if you tell yourself the secrets you've been keeping?

_____
_____
_____
_____
_____
_____

HELPING OTHERS
DO WHAT THEY CAN

Moral mandates have always helped to govern human behavior. Civilizations have consistently deemed such codes helpful, knowing full well that chaos would result without them.

As I comment in the book, these codes frequently consist of prohibitions and proscriptions—thou shalt not do this or that. Individual choice was seldom stressed. The desired behaviors weren't exactly optional. Even though there was an historical concurrent strain of thinking that emphasized behavior based on choice, not coercion, it was not widely observed.

Along came Jesus, and things changed—for good. He urged his followers to adhere to the Golden Rule—"Do unto others as you would have them do unto you"—and, from that moment on, human beings became more aware that, indeed, they really did have a choice regarding how to live and behave.

Behavior was not just based on moral admonitions: it was now understood to also be communally constructed with implications for personal fulfillment through social give-and-take. The true meaning of one's personal life became inextricably interwoven with the lives of everyone else in the community. Each person's purpose became intimately involved with other people. The selfishness inherent in every human being was transformed into a vital means for personal wholeness.

Although to live by such words takes courage and commitment, it's at least a progression toward your better Self when you—against all odds—make the right choice. Your better Self grows through a succession—a progression—of kind and empathetic deeds that you can do *voluntarily*.

> **Exercise:** List three specific ways that you've helped other people accomplish what they never thought they could—but that *you* knew they could? What caused you to help them in these ways? How did you feel when you did? What happened to the people you helped—a month after you helped them? Were they still able—or perhaps even more able—to do on their own what you helped them do earlier? In other words, did their better Selves "stick?" How can you ensure that YOUR better Self sticks around for the long haul?

_____

_____

Emerson was right: "Trust men and they will be true to you; treat them greatly and they will show themselves great." Your better Self becomes great by treating others greatly. How are you treating others today?

RE-MEMBER

To remember is to call up out of your memories, to experience them again. We've been remembering since we were small children, perhaps toddlers barely aware of our surroundings.

Your past is what Jung might have called "your personal collective unconscious," millions of individual memories serving as the framework of your life. Most of us remain unaware that we have control over the way we "call up" our memories—the manner in which we access and arrange them to construct our self-portraits and, therfore, how we see our potential to become our better Selves.

A fortunate few possess memories of early childhood that fill them with a warm glow. Childhood should be like that for all of us—a foundation of positive memories shaped by loved ones who cared about us and made that caring known through their selfless love.

But what if it isn't? What if your earliest memories, and also a lot of the succeeding ones, weren't very nice? I know a man whose mother tried to drown him like an unwanted kitten when he was a child of four. Does he hate the world he's a part of and live his life burdened by a haze of bitterness and spite?

No, he's one of the most positive and upbeat persons I know. He's learned a great trick—more valuable than any "magic bullets" on the market today—of how to re-arrange his memories in different ways—often very different than how they must have seemed to him long ago—and to practice the art of memory re-interpretation. By re-membering his past, he has severed the causal link that so many of us blindly accept as naturally existing between the past and the present. By re-membering, he has freed his future from the tyranny of his past.

This man told me that he deliberately re-interprets his past in the light of new information—a constant flood of new memories that he's making every waking moment. He's become adept at using these memories to add new perspectives to whatever he may once have known and felt. He is no longer merely acquiescing to the influence his past has on his present but is intentionally working it the other way around, too, by choosing to re-member his past with the assistance of his present experiences.

Is he deluded? Perhaps he's forgotten how to be truly sad—especially when he meets his better Self just around each corner of his mind through his practice of re-membering.

Recall a particularly distasteful experience. What are the emotions that you're feeling as you remember it? Now, ask yourself, "What else could this mean?" and "How else could I feel about it?"
Try this to help you get started in the process of re-membering. Make a large dot in the center of a clean piece of paper, like this:

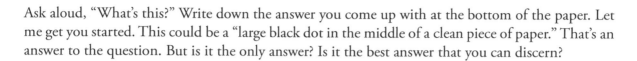

Ask aloud, "What's this?" Write down the answer you come up with at the bottom of the paper. Let me get you started. This could be a "large black dot in the middle of a clean piece of paper." That's an answer to the question. But is it the only answer? Is it the best answer that you can discern?

Next ask, "What's another answer?" Be creative. Apply no filters in your thinking. Each time you answer the question, add it to the list at the bottom of the page and then ask the question again, "What's another answer?" Keep at it until you have a list of at least *ten* answers.

When you do this exercise, you'll find that a single experience can yield multiple meanings, each with powerful insights about better ways to make decisions and live your life. This applies equally to experiences in the present and the past.

Exercise 1: Read the following excerpt from an article in a recent Wall Street Journal and then answer the questions at the end.

"The latest research is based on a radical rethinking of how memories are stored in the brain. Scientists used to believe memories are like snapshots on which the details are fixed once they're recorded. Now, many experts accept the view that memories are stored like individual files on a shelf; each time they are pulled down for viewing, they can be altered before being put back into storage. Altering a memory during the time it is off the shelf can create an updated memory that can be saved in place of the old one, scientists believe." (Wall Street Journal, March 16, 2010—Section D1).

Do you believe YOU can do this with your own memories? If you do, will this be an effective tool to help you become—and remain YOUR better Self? How do you do it? Pull an unpleasant memory off the shelf of your mind and ask, "What else could this memory have meant? What else was going on at the time this memory was formed? What could this memory look and feel like from another person's perspective whom I recall being part of it? Does this memory have anything to do with how I see myself—and how I live my life and perform my work—today?

_____

_____

_____

_____

_____

_____

Exercise 2: Recall an experience you had that was painful. When you remember it, do you still feel twinges of discomfort? If so, why do you think you do? Do you want to keep re-feeling the pain? If not, what can you do to make it stop?

_____

_____

_____

_____

_____

_____

Exercise 3: Once an event occurs, the accompanying emotions can be re-felt when the event is recalled in memory. This can be either pleasant or painful. Unfortunately, it seems to be a human trait to dwell on past pain thinking that, if we do so enough times, we'll finally succeed at "rewriting" our personal history thereby making it more pleasant. Do you think this is possible to do? Have you ever tried it? What were the results?

_____

_____

_____

_____

_____

_____

BE REMINDED

Sometimes we do forget who we are. Our lives can somehow evolve into a recurring experience, as in Bill Murray's famous movie, "Groundhog Day," where déjà vu kept happening again and again (get it?). In these circumstances, one day seems to merge into another and they all seem wearily alike. In retrospect, our lives seem to rush by and we have little to show for our "living."

> **Exercise 1**: The humorist, Erma Bombeck, quipped, "The problem with life is that it's so . . . daily!" What do you think she meant? What implications for your own life might this have for you? Can you live any more than a single day at a time?

_____

_____

_____

_____

_____

_____

It's easy to forget our wholeness and lose sight of our better Selves in a fog of our own making. Just as Simba, in the animated movie, "The Lion King," lapses from his better Self, so can we.

Lapsing is so common that, throughout our lives, we are all more than what we have become. Worn down by life's tribulations, we forget. Allow yourself to be reminded of who you truly are—of what you have been and what you can become.

How have you lapsed from the reality of your better Self that you once experienced—perhaps long ago—perhaps just recently? Is there a common theme in the stories of your lapses that might indicate specifically how you've been sabotaging your efforts to become—and remain—your better Self?

_____

_____

_____

_____

_____

_____

_____

In the space below, write your story of being reminded of your better Self. Who reminded you? What did they say and do that brought your better Self more clearly into view? What were your initial reactions when you heard that you had a better Self?

_____
_____
_____
_____
_____
_____
_____

Exercise 2: Who will you ask to remind you of who you can become or who you have been—your better Self—at those times when you have forgotten? Seek out those persons and ask them to hold you accountable to your better Self. Some losses are worse than others. When you lose sight of your better Self, you need others to remind you that you have done just that. Listen to them. They want you to be whole and peaceful. Don't' you?

_____
_____
_____
_____
_____
_____

Exercise 3: Consider how you have lapsed from the person that you once were. Is this the person you want to be again today? Would that person deal with your current circumstances any better than you're dealing with them now? Could you become an even better person than your "past persona?" How? If you can't answer this question re-read the book and this study guide! Your answers will become apparent.

_____
_____
_____
_____
_____
_____

ALONE BUT NOT LONELY

Henry David Thoreau wasn't alone in his thoughts about our being alone. Millions have rued their lives of quiet desperation, in moments of disquieting reflection, as if gazing through a glass darkly.

Those afflicted with Asperger's Syndrome, a form of high-functioning autism, experience a sense of isolation on a daily basis. These unfortunate people, because their brains are "wired differently" causing them to somehow miss the non-verbal sensory cues and "body language" of others they happen to be with, may appear to lack empathy. They feel alone in the midst of other people.

Do you have a sense of being "inside" a body that completely *confines* you but that doesn't completely *define* you? You have a body, but you're more than that. And you know it.

Exercise 1: When did you first realize that you were not the only thing in the world worth others' time, attention and love? How did you react to learning that? Was it as traumatic as when you first learned that Santa Claus, the Tooth Fairy and the Easter Bunny were really one and the same person? They aren't???

_____

_____

_____

_____

_____

_____

Exercise 2: Read my story of hiking in the Rocky Mountains below. Recall a time when you were all alone and needed help. Perhaps your life was in danger. How did you feel? What did you do to deal with your situation? Whatever you did, it obviously worked because you're reading this now. How did you react when finally another human being showed up?

I started out late one glorious summer morning to hike a remote trail in the Colorado Rocky Mountains. I was unprepared to undertake such a trek because I didn't really know how long the trail was. Nevertheless, in my youthful sense of invincibility, I thought I could finish by sundown. As it turned out, it was almost twenty-four miles—up and down steep and occasionally rugged terrain. I discovered later that the trail went through black bear country. I never saw anyone along the way—fortunately, including black bears.

About three hours into the hike, I got very thirsty. I had no water with me—but the trail ran parallel to—and very high above—a large lake. When I could stand my thirst no longer, I made my way down to the lake and, cupping my hands, scooped up some water to take into my parched mouth. I'll never forget how the water tasted—like gasoline! I could barely keep it in my mouth much less swallow it. But swallow it I would have to do if I wanted to remain hydrated enough to get to the end of the trail.

After about four hours, my hips began to hurt with every step, which helped take my mind off my plaguing thirst and the pain in my feet that had begun an hour before. A couple of hours later darkness began to fall and with it the cold began to set in. I was not dressed for such an adventure. I knew that if I stopped, I would get too cold to continue so I kept trudging and plodding believing that I would get to the end of the trail even though I really had no idea how much farther that might actually be.

Even though I knew the friend who had dropped me off at the trailhead would call for help when I didn't arrive at the designated time, I nevertheless felt very alone, and lonely. If I were going to make it, I would have to rely solely on myself.

There are some mighty strange and frightening sounds that erupt in the Rockies at night! Each sound provided increasing motivation for me to continue walking! I eventually arrived at the trail's end nearly twelve hours after I had started. As I emerged from the forest, a ranger shone a flashlight in my direction. He asked, "Mr. Wallace?" My sense of relief was palpable. But my sense of accomplishment was even greater because on that trail my better Self was tried and found true.

_____

_____

_____

_____

_____

_____

Exercise 3: Try to remember the last time you felt lonely. Were you alone at that moment? What made you feel lonely, especially if you weren't alone?

_____

_____

_____

_____

_____

_____

Exercise 4: Imagine that your better Self lies just beyond a giant door. You unlatch the handle, push, and swing the door open on its creaking hinges. You step forward to face your better Self. Who do you see looking back at you as you gaze upon a face you think you might recognize? What are its features? Is it smiling? Is this person the "new" you or the "old" you? Who would you rather meet just beyond that giant door?

If you're not living as your better Self right now, do you believe that it is not very far away—just on the other side of the door of your heart—and that you can open that door any time you want? A door divides one space from another. Do you have any "doors" inside you? Why? What parts of yourself have you arranged into separate compartments? Why?

_____

_____

_____

_____

_____

_____

The Meaning of Monday

For many of us, Monday ushers in a new work week. After a weekend "off" and away from the stresses and strains of the work week, Monday seems like a synonym for drudgery and de-motivation. Monday can be a daunting thought on Sunday evenings.

Monday can also translate into the plaintive cries of millions: "Must I always work in this job to earn my livelihood? Isn't there a better way?" There is always a better way for your better Self!

It starts with how you view "Monday." If your recent past is filled with fearful imaginings of what may happen tomorrow, the dread you experience occurs because of a poor envisioning process. This means that you have not taken control of visualizing what you WANT to happen tomorrow—you're just fearing that what does happen tomorrow won't be what you want, even though you haven't clearly decided what you want.

When we go to the movies, we have no difficulty suspending our disbelief that what we're seeing on the screen is mere fantasy and only a version of someone else's visualized reality.

Why not treat Mondays (and every other day!) as a "screen" or a "palette" upon which you project and paint the reality you want to experience on that day? By visualizing and then projecting that "reality" into the future you are actually predicting *your* future in a startlingly unambiguous way.

Suddenly it doesn't matter anymore that it's Monday on your doorstep. Instead, Monday beckons you to experience what you know is going to happen because your better Self has already "screened the scenes."

> **Exercise:** Take a seat. Think about tomorrow. Can you see your better Self there? What is it doing? How is it acting? What is it saying and feeling? Who is it interacting with? What is happening in the morning, the afternoon and at the end of the day? Is it Monday tomorrow—or does it really matter anymore what day of the week it is?

LET IT UP

I've shared my summer camp experiences at Little Grassy Lake in Southern Illinois. Playing "Keep Away" with a beach ball in the lake's swimming area had me sitting on the ball, which sounds more painful than it was.

Why would I want to hide the ball from the other team? Because they wanted what I had, but I didn't want them to see that I had it. Often, whenever you try to hide something, others can sense it and will become quite curious to know what you're hiding from them. Consequently, you will have to spend time and energy keeping it stuffed down and out of sight. This robs you of much of what you need to become your better Self.

Keeping unpleasant and distasteful experiences and memories beneath the surface of your consciousness means that you have less energy for your relationships and the work of self-examination. It takes your focus off the activities that lead to achieving your worthy aspirations.

Dostoyevsky's glimpses into our interior worlds imply that to keep secrets from others—and ourselves—is a common thread through humanity. But secrets, no matter how necessary it might be for our survival to keep them, are best revealed at some point before we die. Otherwise, kept hidden, they become the source of a "living death."

Some secrets should be shared cautiously, a very few not at all. But if we can let it up, allowing a heretofore hidden secret to enter our consciousness and even be shared with a trusted person, it can feel liberating—and seldom fails to reveal significant aspects of our better Self.

No secrets should ever be kept from yourself. Those that you do keep from yourself become hindrances to manifesting your worthy aspirations and impediments to becoming your better Self.

> **Exercise 1**: How is it possible to hide something from yourself? What has worked for you in the past? Are you still hiding something from long ago? How do you feel about continuing to stuff it down? What might help you let it up—today?

_____

_____

_____

_____

_____

_____

Exercise 2: What's the biggest secret you've ever kept from others? From yourself? Have you released your emotional and mental grip on it yet and revealed it to anyone? If so, how did that make you feel? If not, how does keeping it hidden make you feel? Is your life getting any better by keeping it "stuffed down?"

_____

_____

_____

_____

_____

_____

LET IT GO

My story about when I learned how to pray, in what is today often called middle school, but in those days was simply 'junior high,' and how my prayers were answered in a way that I never would have expected, sets the stage for how we can be liberated from the confines of misunderstanding.

Misunderstandings are like weeds in the fields of our minds. They must be tended to or they will take over the fertile fields of our thoughts and worthy aspirations. People have said things about us since we were old enough to listen and understand. But not only do we sometimes misinterpret what is said about us, oft-times what is said was never true about us in the first place—or else contained just a few grains of truth mixed in with shovelfuls of half-truths or careless and inaccurate observations.

More often than not, what is said to you about you has more to do with the speaker than with you. Keep that in mind when you re-member your wounding memories no matter when they occurred in your life. If we continue to be troubled by someone else's hurtful words or opinions long after they're hurled at us, then that says more about you than the speaker.

Why would you want to repeatedly inflict an old injury on yourself? It's because you are not letting go of the pain perhaps because you have grown used to it, like a pebble in your shoe that you learn to ignore even though it continues to cause discomfort. You have covered up your better Self with "comfortable misery." But it's time to let it go.

Bend over, take off your shoe, remove the pebble and get on with your life. You'll find your pace is quicker and your step is livelier. Let go of your grip on wounding memories, regardless of how they happened—by means of a simple misunderstanding or as a result of malicious intent. Let go by re-membering in a manner that is kinder to yourself and that takes the truth of your potential more seriously.

We come into contact with many people during our lives—some of them well-meaning, some of them not so well-meaning; some are so self-absorbed or even evil as to be of no use in guiding us toward our better Selves. Instead, they will seek to divert us away from our better Selves. Don't let them do it! Let them go!

When we continue to allow wounds to fester in the sanctuaries of our memory, it's a lot like drinking poison. Rather than cling to toxic thoughts, memories or people, it's much better to let it go. Words like "forgiveness" and "reconciliation" are made real when you are able to let it go. Otherwise, they remain just words.

Should you always forgive, even when people you know commit the greatest of evils and show not the slightest twinge of remorse? In some grievous instances it can be most difficult to do. But the greater risk can mean the greatest reward in the fast lane toward a better you. In most cases, the act of "letting go" releases the dead weight in your mind and causes your better Self to rise faster to the surface for everyone to see.

Exercise 1: What are you holding on to that is actually dragging you down and holding you back? Why are you still holding on? What can you do to let it go—for good—today? It doesn't have to be hard—only as hard as you want to make it.

_____

_____

_____

_____

_____

_____

Exercise 2: How have you been misunderstood? How have you misunderstood others? What were the consequences of these misunderstandings? In what ways did you build your self-image on what you now know were misunderstandings? How have you been able to alter how you see yourself based on new information about the past?

_____

_____

_____

_____

_____

_____

Exercise 3: Are there any pebbles in your shoes? What are they? Why are they still there? Why don't you take them out? Are they slowing you down from achieving your worthy aspirations? How?

_____

_____

_____

_____

_____

_____

Exercise 4: If you've ever done so, do you recall how you felt when you let an emotional burden go? How did you life change afterward?

_____

_____

_____

_____

_____

_____

CONFIDENCE

Without confidence, we don't have much. As I've said, the word 'confidence' is derived from its Latin roots meaning "unified trust" or "belief," as when someone believes in you. Having someone believe in us is like a pleasant warm wind filling our sails and gently moving us onward to our better Selves.

A girl was climbing a steep hill. She climbed higher and higher. "I'll never reach the top," she said out loud, struggling with every step. She thought she was alone on the mountain, but she wasn't. Peering out from behind a crag was a kindly talking mountain moose. Such creatures are relatively rare.

"I heard that," said the moose, "but you're wrong."

"I'm wrong?" said the girl, immediately recognizing the moose from pictures in a book that her father had read to her as a small child. The name of the book was, "Who's Your Moose?"

"Yes," said the moose. "You *will* reach the top."

"I'm so tired," said the girl. "*How* can I reach the top?"

"How?" the moose repeated. "Just keep on climbing. You've come this far and not even being tired can stop you now. I'm only a talking moose but I know *that* much!"

The girl kept on climbing, huffing and puffing, but now believing without a doubt that she could—and would reach the summit. The girl's moose believed in her abilities and provided her with some much-needed confidence.

> **Exercise 1**: Who is YOUR moose? How many moose (or is that, 'meese?') do you have? What are their names? Call one of them and thank them for being your moose. That should be fun!

> _____
> _____
> _____
> _____
> _____
> _____

Confidence is a vital ingredient in successfully beginning, pursuing and completing difficult undertakings. Lack of confidence is the primary reason for lack of implementation of good ideas.

If we delve into the etymology of the English word "confidence," we find that the prefix, "con," is Latin meaning "with" or "together." The root, "fido," translates into "trust," "believe," "confide in." Whenever you see an English word that begins with "con" or "com" it very often indicates that the original meaning of the word involved a concept that was communally formed: the word was intended to convey that other people were inextricably interwoven in what happens to the individual.

We often refer to "self-confidence." However, according to this analysis, this term is actually a redundancy. The word confidence is sufficient to express one's positive attitude toward personal competence, capability and self-sufficiency. The word confidence literally means to trust or believe together with others in an interdependent community. An individual will find it difficult to be confident without the positive input and support from others.

The existence of confidence in any member of a community indicates that that community has an established culture of mutual trust and respect among its citizens. This does not necessarily hold true for all cultures and communities that a person happens to be a part of.

For instance, you could be totally confident of yourself within your home environment but totally lacking in confidence within any number of other organizations and associations of which you are a member. This has as much to do with the kinds of input from others in these respective environments as it does with one's membership qualifications of family, ability, preparation, experience or knowledge, for example.

We weave our personal realities mainly from the multiple inputs from others.

A boy was struggling to move a large rock. His father walked by and asked, "Son, are you using all your strength to move that rock?"

The boy replied, "Yes, Dad."

His father retorted, "Son, you are not using all your strength because you have not yet asked me to help you."

Our strength and personal realities are formed and sustained by the contributions from others. We are not nearly so strong or confident without them. When others are encouraging and supportive, confidence builds and you are more likely to stretch as well as strengthen your talents and abilities toward successful and innovative applications and outcomes.

When You Know You Know

One of the ways a community demonstrates its support for its individual members is to provide solid practical information regarding what it takes to succeed within the community and beyond. The knowledge that is passed down and around becomes the foundation for an individual's confidence in making decisions and behaving in ways that are conducive for success.

After this knowledge is disseminated, the supportive community will then provide practical opportunities for the individual to apply what was learned. These experiences create an internal sense of what works and what doesn't work.

When you know you know how to succeed, your confidence in performing the necessary tasks that lead to successful achievement soars. Your confidence helps you assess risks realistically and to bounce back from failure quickly.

Becoming Confident in All You Do

How do you become confident in all the situations in your life? It's simple, really. You give to others what you want them to give to you. Life echoes. It ripples. What you give out you get back in waves.

Although confidence is socially constructed, the individual has a large part to play in creating a community environment in which confidence is engendered and nurtured. Mahatma Gandhi wisely observed, "You must be the change you wish to see in the world." I would paraphrase this slightly to make it more immediate to one's personal environment and also say, "you must be the change you wish to see in others." If you wish to be around people who smile more, then smile more! If you want to work in an environment that is characterized by teamwork and mutual respect, then demonstrate to others how these characteristics can be embodied and pragmatically expressed on a consistent basis.

I realize that to adopt this approach is to invite the possibility of failure, perhaps even ridicule. Life is full of risks. It certainly is a risk, albeit rather innocuous in nature, to smile at someone who clearly is in no mood to smile. They might scowl back! Then how would you feel? But it's not about how you feel. It's about how you act.

If you want to be around people who have more reasons to smile then you should take the risk that the smile you offer will not be returned at that very moment. You might feel awkward and uncomfortable. Big deal! By smiling, even when you don't feel like it, you're giving permission for others to do the same, if not now then later. You're setting the stage for their subsequent behavior toward you and others not just their immediate reaction to your current behavior.

Helen Keller, who had more reasons than anybody else in history to be grumpy and sad, nonetheless proclaimed, "Be happy. Talk happiness. Happiness calls out responsive gladness in others."

Changing Others By Changing Yourself

You've no doubt heard that you can only change yourself and not others. This is true if you try to change someone else's behavior without first trying to change your own.

It has been my experience that you can, in fact, alter others' ways of acting by altering your own first, just as Gandhi noted. William James, pragmatist philosopher & psychologist (1842—1910) said, "the greatest discovery of my generation is that human beings can alter their lives by altering their attitudes of mind." I would go further and say that human beings can alter other people's lives by altering their own personal attitudes of mind, as I've described above.

When you change your attitude of mind, that is, the way you habitually think (an attitude is nothing more than a habit of thought), then you alter the way you behave and this, in turn, alters the ways others behave toward you.

There are two ways to change yourself that will also result in changes in others. When you change something about yourself, especially your behavior, others are naturally challenged to change their responses to the "new you."

By changing yourself you are also altering the social environment from which you receive your cues and clues about how to be confident. In effect, you are setting up a "virtuous cycle" (as opposed to a "vicious cycle") that creates the conditions for perpetual mutual benefit for both the individual and the community.

Here are the two ways to change yourself:

- *Think your way into a new way of acting*

- *Act your way into a new way of thinking*

It's true that habitual behavior stems from habitual thought and that the quality of your actions flow from the quality of your thinking. This is the "garbage in—garbage out," "excellence in—excellence out" notion in behavioral psychology. Thinking your way into a new way of acting is effective. However, it often takes a long time because you must think the new thought repetitively in order for it to erase and replace the old way of thinking and for this new way to finally change your behavior. Often there is not enough time to allow for this way of changing to work itself out.

More immediate change can be achieved by simply acting the way you want others to behave. It's a curious fact of life that by doing something, even if you don't feel like doing it, you make it easier to do again. Smiling elicits a desire, no matter how small or subconscious, to have reason to continue smiling. Treating co-workers as colleagues of equal worth even if they aren't of equal status creates in their minds a reason to want to collaborate with you in the future.

This sort of "risky behavior" engenders trust and tames the tentativeness toward teamwork because it results in the experience of mutual respect that fosters the desire to repeat the behavior. The action gives rise to the thinking that guides and supports future actions. This is the "virtuous cycle" out of which confidence and achievement flow.

"Be Sure You're Right, Then Go Ahead"

General Robert E. Lee, widely respected for his military and personal leadership, said, "You have only always to do what is right. It will become easier by practice, and you enjoy in the midst of your trials the pleasure of an approving conscience."

As a young child, I listened to the song of the story of Davy Crockett countless times while sitting on the floor of my bedroom in front of my little record player. I recall the spoken words that immediately preceded the beginning of the song. "Be sure you're right, then go ahead." This was Crockett's philosophy of life. It was his personal motto. It shaped his behavior and tuned his integrity throughout his life.

Doing "only always" what you're sure is right is the only true source of confidence. When you possess "the pleasure of an approving conscience" in all that you do, you feed your soul with the necessary nutrient that keeps it strong, resolute and successful, even in failure. We esteem General Lee today because of his strength of confidence, character and wisdom even though he failed to win a great war that he believed was right to fight.

Doing right means that you do things you don't always feel like doing. It means that you do things you don't have to do. But it's precisely these things that determine what you'll be able to do more easily and with greater impact in the future.

Doing right creates the inspiration to continue to do right and the confidence that you are doing right. The great early twentieth century composer, Igor Stravinsky, said, "Just as appetite comes by eating, so work brings inspiration, if inspiration is not discernible at the beginning."

Self-Made Communities Count, Too

We can now say with confidence that community, within which confidence is born, is not merely something into which one is born and therefore has no control over. It can be more than that.

A community can be formed in the mind of an individual by means of reading and meditating. We learn how to be confident from the mental and spiritual communities we form throughout our lives as well as the physical communities of family, neighborhood, city, school, church, synagogue, mosque, associations and job. And we have control over these inner communities in that we can continually modify our sources of wisdom and understanding of what is right and worthy of our efforts.

Getting It Right From the Start

Confidence is telling the truth in advance of experiencing it. You can lead with confidence when you start something even if you've never done it before because your confidence is a predictor of the successful completion of the endeavor.

Confidence is a term to describe belief in one's ability to succeed in life. William James comes again to aid our understanding: "Our belief at the beginning of a doubtful undertaking is the one thing that insures the successful outcome of our venture." And again, "Be not afraid of life. Believe that life is worth living, and your belief will help create the fact."

In the September 22, 2006 issue of the USA Today newspaper, an article on the "soul of a champion" quotes Patrick Cohn, sports psychologist and President of Peak Performance Sports, on the need for confidence in order to attain championship levels of performance. "Self-confidence is probably the number one mental skill that championship athletes possess. Simply put, it is their belief in their ability to perform. They see themselves as winners." Confidence is seeing yourself as successfully accomplishing something you haven't yet done, bringing that future positive self-image into the present and then using it as the impetus and inspiration to succeed at doing it.

So Then, It Works Both Ways

Confidence arises from and is fed by both the past and the future. It begins in the communities that the individual participates in, both visible and invisible. It is nurtured by history and visualization, by experience and expectation, by fact and dream, by knowledge and hope, by achievement and aspiration.

Acquiring and growing confidence is the responsibility of each individual. You are in charge of how confidently you feel and act by choosing what to focus on in your past and in your future.

If you're sure you're right in your focus, you'll be sure to bring about what you're thinking about. And the realization of this confidence will contribute to the community the confidence others need to do what they're sure is right. And thus the virtuous cycle is formed that results in increasingly greater achievements and benefits for humanity and the world.

> **Exercise 2**: What other "com" and "con" English words can you think of? After writing them down, think about how their respective meanings involve social input.

> **Exercise 3**: *"The Social Construction of Reality"* is the name of a seminal book by Peter L. Berger and Thomas Lucian, published in 1966. The central idea is that people interacting together in a society over time form mental representations of each other's actions. These concepts eventually become mutually expected habits of thought and behavior. Every generation of new people eventually adopts an institutionalized notion of these common expectations thereby embedding meaning in the society itself. Therefore, "reality" is said to be socially constructed.

> Do you agree with this theory? Does it make sense that we are all a part of each other's "reality" and that we each have a hand in constructing what others believe to be their reality? If this is true, what does this mean for the way you live the rest of your life?

_____

_____

_____

_____

Exercise 4: Recall a time in school when the teacher asked a question of the class and you knew you knew the right answer. How did you feel? Didn't you shoot your hand up as fast as you could, maybe even wave it around to attract the teacher's attention so you could be called on to show that you knew the right answer? When you know you know the right answer, aren't you filled with confidence and boldness to proceed immediately toward implementing your knowledge? How are you implementing your knowledge today in ways that will move you closer to manifesting your worthy aspirations? Are you excited to do so? Why aren't you doing it right now?

_____

_____

_____

_____

_____

_____

Exercise 5: When were you ridiculed for acting bold or unconventional? Did you take it personally? How did you deal with it? Did you "cave" or did you persevere? Did this experience strengthen or weaken your determination to achieve your goal? Did you allow what others were saying to get in your way of seeing clearly what you wanted to accomplish?

_____

_____

_____

_____

_____

_____

Exercise 6: If you already know what you need to know to get what you want in life, and if you already possess the strength necessary to accomplish you goals, then why don't you have everything you want right now?

"The difference between a successful person and others is not a lack of strength, not a lack of knowledge, but rather in a lack of will."—Vincent T. Lombardi

Do you agree? Why? What one thing can you do today to increase your will to win?

_____

_____

_____

_____

_____

_____

Exercise 7: How do you know when you're right? What feelings accompany such inner certainty? Are you always sure you're right before you take action? What were some of the results when you did something without knowing (or feeling) you were right?

_____

_____

_____

_____

_____

_____

Exercise 8: What do you think about General Lee's comments? Can you "always do what is right?" What happens when you're wrong?

_____

_____

_____

_____

_____

_____

Exercise 9: What is your personal motto? Do you have one? If so, do you really believe it? Do you refer to it before making any decision? Why have a motto at all?

_____

_____

_____

_____

_____

Exercise 10: When was the last time you did something nice for someone you didn't "have" to do? How did that make you feel? Do you like doing what you don't have to do? What would cause you to do it again?

_____
_____
_____
_____
_____
_____

Exercise 11: "Confidence is telling the truth before experiencing it." Do you agree with this statement? What does it mean for your next undertaking? For the next decision you make?

_____
_____
_____
_____
_____
_____

Exercise 12: How have others helped you become confident and successful in dealing with difficult situations? How have you helped others become confident? What else can you do?

_____
_____
_____
_____
_____
_____

Exercise 13: "You bring about what you think about." Another way of putting this is what the famous motivator, Earl Nightingale, called the "strangest secret," "You become what you think about." Do you agree?

In what ways have you experienced the truth of this idea? Do you believe that if you changed your thinking you would eventually change your reality?

_____
_____
_____
_____
_____
_____

ASSUMPTIONS

When I was a very young boy, and first heard the word "paradox," I assumed that it meant "a pair of docks," although I wasn't quite sure what that meant. It sounded a lot like a "pair of socks" so I assumed that I could wear a paradox on my feet.

By the time I was an adult, and was about to deliver my first sermon, "The Great Paradox of Life," I was on to different assumptions. One such assumption was that "paradox is paramount," which had nothing to do with a pair of mountains. Another assumption was that everyone in my congregation knew what the word "paradox" meant.

Assumptions are presumptive by their very nature. To extrapolate beyond the moment, beyond the present instant you are living, always entails some risk. Assuming that anything about your point of view is simultaneously etched in the mind of another is risky because it deprives you of knowing what others really are thinking—a knowledge that is often needed to help you advance toward your better Self.

We really can't help projecting our thoughts onto others, injecting our viewpoints into their unique consciousness. We do this as a way to make sense of our world—and to try to control it. But to do so blithely and without awareness that we are, in fact, doing it can be outright dangerous. It leads to missteps, miscommunication and mistakes. Assumptions can lead us to miss becoming our better Selves.

Unconsciously making assumptions impedes your worthy aspirations. We often believe that something outside ourselves is blocking our path toward our better Self, but often it's just an assumption we've been making about what others are thinking and how they see the world.

When you assume something that isn't true, your assumption acts as a self-imposed limitation. ***Barriers to your better Self are never externally created.***

> **Exercise 1**: What assumptions are you making right now that might be interfering with your efforts to manifest your worthy aspirations and hindering you from becoming your better Self? Assumptions are nothing more than filling in the blank parts of your knowledge and experience with something you believe—or hope to be true. What if it's not true? What can you do to "fill in the blank" with more factual and accurate data so that what you believe to be true is actually true— for you and others?

_____

_____

_____

_____

_____

_____

Exercise 2: Barriers to your better Self are never externally created. What does this mean? Do you believe this? If not, why not?

_____

_____

_____

_____

_____

INVITATIONS

Living in these tumultuous times, NOT being knowledgeable and informed socially and politically can cause us to be justifiably accused of "hiding our heads in the sand." However, an endless diet of pundits and commentary is enough to obscure anything that actually *happens*, perhaps beyond recognition of the true facts. Being "oversaturated" with the news often results in rude behavior that seeks to overwhelm others with your own point of view to the exclusion of honest dialogue, mutual understanding and respect.

We can accept these invitations to become obsessed with certain sensationalized facets of our NOW. Or we can politely refuse.

Techno-gadgets, such as cell phones and computers emerge as our children's "toys." "Texting" is as ubiquitous these days as lightening bugs in June. We are becoming closer to our "techno-friends" than our human (and non-human) friends because, even though they are merely the means by which we stay in touch with our friends, we grow increasingly attached to them because we spend so much time using them.

A lot of this activity is negativity, certain to distance you from your better Self. But again, you have a CHOICE. Don't extend the invitation to have this inane clutter and attachment to things occupy the space between your ears. Treat it for what it is—an invading army. It doesn't belong inside you—don't pay it any of your mind—or at least not as much as it seems to greedily demand.

Focusing too much on current events too often causes us to overlook the larger contexts of history and human nature within which they occur. The "news" isn't really new; no matter what, when, where or how the news is published, it always portrays similar themes of humanity. The same old stories about *us*, however, don't have to be the same old stories about *YOU*. Your better Self writes its own history and invites others to view their own in different and more empowering ways.

> **Exercise 1**: Have you ever "texted" or done "email" on your cell phone while driving? While in a meeting? Have you done so while in a conversation on another phone? While in a conversation face-to-face? What is so much more important in the phone than "in your face?"

_____

_____

_____

_____

_____

Exercise 2: What invitations are you accepting that are being extended by the technology surrounding you? Are these liberating you to pursue your worthy aspirations, or are they actually constraining you? What invitations are you accepting by others to engage in certain types of behavior that will move you closer to your better Self—or further away? What invitations are you issuing to others that will help them compose and tell their own stories as their better Selves?

_____

_____

_____

_____

_____

_____

UNPLANNED INFLUENCE

It is important to understand that every physical thing outside yourself can serve as an extension of yourself. One of the primary subjects of the study of primitive civilizations is how people discovered and used tools to get things done. Tools can reduce the amount of time and effort it takes to accomplish tasks necessary for human survival and development.

Technology is just another name for tools. Just as we use a long stick to retrieve a wayward Frisbee from its perch high in a tree, so, too, we use a computer, as I am right now, to capture and arrange our thoughts to better communicate them to others. Although the two are quite different in capabilities and content, their functions are identical—helping human beings to accomplish their aims efficiently.

Sometimes the tools we use are the right ones for the job. Other times, they aren't. Knowing which tools to use is an important part of your better Self.

But your better Self also knows that tools aren't the only means by which things get done. The Scottish poet, Robert Burns, famously penned, "The best laid plans of mice and men oft go astray." You may plan to use certain of your tools and resources to influence the outcomes of the events in your life, but it doesn't always work out.

In the case of the tool of my cell phone and my mother overhearing my prayer with a dying woman, it wasn't the tool that influenced the outcome—it was the unpretentious presence of my better Self that the tool conveyed. The unplanned "accidental" influences exerted by your better Self are much more powerful than any plans you make or any tools you use to make something happen.

> **Exercise:** What are the tools you use that help you accomplish what you want to achieve? How are you using them? Could you accomplish the same things without these tools using only the power of your better Self? When have you influenced others to become their better Selves—and you didn't know it until after it had happened? How did you exert your influence?

_____
_____
_____
_____
_____

A Better World

The greatest threat to the entire universe as conceived in the TV series, "Star Trek: The Next Generation," was the "Borg," a mindless amorphous mass of mechanical predatory beings whose only purpose was to traverse the universe to absorb and incorporate every living thing into its lifeless "collective."

Its modus operandi was to assimilate living beings into its commune by gradually turning them into machines with robotic allegiance to the corporate mission. It was relentless and untiring. Its enemy was individuality. There was no such thing as a better Self—only a single Self with no self-awareness. The Borg's battle cry was, "Resistance is futile."

Your life is part of a world with which you must interact. If you don't actively engage the culture in which you live, it will inexorably consume your individuality and make you just another part of the "collective." But you can resist by connecting with others as your better Self. When you do this, they become aware of their own uniqueness and potential contributions that can make the common "good" even better.

My client enthusiastically believed that "as your people grow, so grows the country and the world." This is not exactly the drumbeat to which most businesses march. It can be risky to focus on helping your people contribute to the greater common good because they just might do it!

A business culture, and more specifically a corporate culture, is exclusive by nature. It is in competition with "outsiders" and helping them become better is not usually in their best interest. But when this is done, a remarkable thing happens: "a rising tide floats all boats," the saying goes, and everyone in the environment is "lifted up" in some way when someone improves their attitude, skill set, knowledge or their awareness of what they can do to live as their better Selves while helping others become their better Selves.

> **Exercise 1**: If you own a business, or if you owned one, what might be some innovative ways you could serve the common good? What can you do on a local, regional, national and global scale? What kind of actions are you prepared to take?

> _____

> _____

> _____

> _____

> _____

Exercise 2: In what ways are you resisting the persistent influence of a culture that seeks to overwhelm your better Self with trivialities, mindless distractions and mundane uniformity? How is this helping make the common good better?

_____
_____
_____
_____
_____
_____

When you reach for something extraordinary, your better Self helps you "make it so."

CREATE THE REALITY
YOU REALLY WANT TO LIVE IN

Emotionally reeling from the comments of ignorant naysayers, we often underestimate ourselves. This happens more when we're young and still trying to prove ourselves, reticent to be too bold, lacking experience, confidence, or both.

Others glimpse only a small facet of what we're capable of doing—and then judge us on a performance in which we've held back the lion's share of our innate talent. Perhaps they're being realistic and are honestly critical of what they see demonstrated, or perhaps they're genuinely wishing us to fail, and are truly being adversarial. In any case, once we incorporate the negative evaluations of someone else, we make the choice to harm ourselves—and we end up diminishing our own abilities.

If we fail to show others what we can do, they will judge us accordingly. But the judgment of others is not what really matters. Feedback and support from others is important, but our self-image is what's crucial when we're talking about our better Selves.

Your self-image is rooted in an understanding of who you think you are and what you believe you're capable of accomplishing and worthy of having. This self-image gets formed in a variety of ways, usually in a haphazard and disjointed manner, with external inputs weighing more heavily in its formation than our own internal assessments. This more often than not results in a poor picture quality made fuzzier by our lack of mental effort to clear it up.

Meander wasn't meandering through philosophical speculation when he quoted the ancient axiom, "Know thyself." He was focused on the essential tools for living well. Self-knowledge is the yardstick that not only permits us to achieve almost anything, but also provides valuable perspective when we fail.

That's another reason why T2 = "Think Time," is important to do as often as you can. The better we know ourselves, the easier we can BE our selves, and potentially our better Selves.

> **Exercise 1**: The Mormons, or Latter Day Saints, keep a tradition called "The Family Home Evening." In this tradition, the entire family gets together at home one evening a week to engage in a wholesome activity. It could be singing songs or playing board games or perhaps chasing squirrels around their backyard picnic table . . . . Could your family organize a regular activity one evening a week? If so, planning is essential, as the activity should be as enjoyable as possible for all. What might be the benefits of regularly having such a family event? If you don't currently have such gatherings, what will you do today to arrange for your first one?

_____

_____

_____

_____

_____

_____

Even if you aren't currently in a family, perhaps a regular get-together with friends or just a single loved one organized for the purpose of bonding and building community might well be advantageous in bringing out your better Selves.

The point is to begin to actively create the reality you really want among those with whom you live. When you are together, you have the opportunities to exercise the tools of your better Self—your words and your thoughts—to shape a reality within which everyone's worthy aspirations can become real and benefit each other.

> **Exercise 2**: In what ways are you consciously shaping the reality your family experiences every day? How are you influencing the ways others work in your job environment? How will you plan to improve the situations—the realities—in which you live and work? What tools could you use to help you plan?

_____

_____

_____

_____

_____

_____

PRACTICE YOUR REALITY

Practice *does* make perfect. We program our brains to accomplish something whenever we practice. Repetition leads to achievement. Your worthy aspirations must be built upon a foundation of practice, transforming them into your reality.

But how much practice is enough?

Basketball legend Michael Jordan would practice dribbling and shooting basketballs into the hoops at the University of North Carolina Athletic Center for 10-12 hours per day. "I got into a routine," he once said in a magazine interview, "and my imagination took over when I made the biggest shots over and over." As a college and pro player, he made many pressure shots over years of top-flight competition. Did Jordan practice enough?

Arnold M. Schopenhauer aspired to win a local greased pig competition. He lived on a 200-acre farm near Calgary, Alberta, where his parents kept two obliging pigs, Tiffany and Malcolm, whom he practiced catching year after year. At the age of thirteen, Arnold caught his first greased pig in a local rodeo competition. He caught many pigs throughout his long life. In fact, he was presented with a lifetime achievement award for catching the most number of greased pigs in the twentieth century.

Catching greased pigs, I suppose, could be a worthy aspiration. It wouldn't be for me. Is it for you? What if Schopenhauer had set loftier aspirations for himself, in the manner of Michael Jordan?

Your aspirations dictate your practice. If he'd made self-mastery his aspiration, he may have realized something more than he eventually did—perhaps he would have practiced his way into his better Self.

"Seeing" is Believing

Visualization is more than a mere suggestion when it comes to practicing the reality you really want to live in. We all have visions of what we want to be, do and have and these are an integral part of your worthy aspirations.

Why does conscious creative visualization work? There are several reasons.

> 1) Regardless of what you are seeking in terms of personal goals, it will be necessary to think about it and create some kind of image or idea of your goal.

> 2) Your subconscious mind is the birthplace for your external reality. It is easiest to understand creative visualization as the "blueprint" stage for making things happen.

As with the construction of a building you must draw a series of detailed pictures before you begin the actual construction. These drawings would include pictures of various aspects of the building: the foundation, electric circuits, plumbing, etc.

3) A model or picture of the completed structure will be presented during this visualization as part of the building process. Without this model any resulting "building" can only be constructed ad hoc and "on the fly." What it winds up looking like is anybody's guess.

Here's how to prepare for creative visualizations that will serve as an effective means for motivating forward toward your better Self:

1) Sit or lie down with your spine straight and close your eyes.

2) Focus your initial attention on your breathing; make it deep, rhythmic and regular.

3) Check in on your body and release any pockets of tension; completely relax every muscle.

Now that you've prepared to visualize creatively, there are four basic steps to making it happen and making it effective.

1) Write down what you would like to accomplish and how you will benefit.

2) Create a mental picture. Don't worry if you can't create an actual image in your mind. Use your imagination as you did when you were a child. Imagine your goal in the present tense as though it already exists. Enlist your five senses when you are visualizing so that you are experiencing the feelings associated with your success. Also, see your desired goal as an observer. Visualize how others will react to your achievement.

3) Practice your visualization often. Make visualization a regular routine. Have fun with it, keep it light and approach it in a relaxed manner.

4) Give your visualization "love." This is the secret ingredient for success with the visualization process. Love is the catalyst that makes everything happen. Love will create an atmosphere of enthusiasm around what you desire and will attract your inner energy to help you manifest your worthy aspirations.

Here's a practical ten-step approach to solving your problems using conscious creative visualization. Use it whenever you feel that your problems are getting you down and seem too tough to manage.

1) Before beginning this visualization write down your problems or areas of concern.

2) Next, write down what you would like to happen or any expectations you would like fulfilled in this situation.

3) Keep a pen and paper next to you.

4) Use the three step preparation technique mentioned above.

5) Visualize a similar problem from the past that had a successful outcome. For example, if you had an interpersonal problem, observe how you worked it out.

6) If you had other similar victories review them also.

7) Re-experience the feelings that you had associated with your emotional state after you succeeded. What positive reactions did you observe around you?

8) See or imagine your present area of concern resolved in the way you would like. What do you hear yourself saying? Experience and enjoy the bodily sensations associated with your victory.

9) Now, open your eyes and quickly take your pen and write down at least five action steps you can take to solve your problem.

10) Finally, write down a specific timetable for taking the above steps.

Near the end of Bruce Lee's famous movie, *"Enter the Dragon,"* the evil antagonist, Han, is taking John Saxon's character on a tour of his collection of feudal weaponry. Han speaks as they walk,

> *"It is difficult to associate these horrors with the proud civilizations that created them. Sparta, Rome, the knights of Europe, the Samurai . . . all shared the lone ideal: the honor or strength, because it is strength that makes all other values possible. Nothing survives without it. Who knows what delicate wonders have died out of the world for want of the strength to survive?"*

In Lee's final copy of the movie script are the following words that were not heard in Han's on-screen soliloquy.

> *"Civilization's highest idea—justice—could not exist without strong men to enforce it. Indeed, what is civilization but simply the honor of strong men? Today, the young are taught nothing of honor. The sense of life as epic, of life as big, of life as something for which one learns to fight—that is foolish to them. To them, grandeur is irrelevant. The young no longer dream."* ("The Art of Expressing the Human Body" compiled and edited by John Little, Tuttle Publishing, 1998, page 26).

Self-discipline is the art of practicing the reality you really want to live in. It is the means of knowing what you can and cannot do and what you will and will not do. This is the definition of ***strength***; it is the dream of an epic life and the grandeur of "living large" in a reality where everyone lives as their better Selves.

Exercise 1: The old maxim sounds correct: "practice makes perfect." Vince Lombardi famously said, "Perfect practice makes perfect." What does it mean to practice "perfectly?" What do you think this means as far as becoming your better Self is concerned?

_____

_____

_____

_____

_____

_____

Exercise 2: Albert Einstein said that the definition of insanity was doing the same thing over and over again but expecting different results. How does this notion fit with Lombardi's? If you do the same thing over and over again, isn't this just another phrase for perfect practice? No matter what you're practicing, even if it's a bad practice, if you do it over and over you'll improve your ability to do it and the resulting outcomes will also get "better." What is more likely to drive you insane is "practicing" nothing in particular, doing the same thing over and over without expecting any results! What do you think?

_____

_____

_____

_____

_____

_____

Exercise 3: I heard of a man who, through his long life, had kept his head down looking for spare change wherever he went. At his death, he had retrieved, by his own accounting, over $5,500 of coins and bills.

Would you spend your life looking for small successes or large ones? What are the large successes you're aiming at? When will you accomplish them? Whose help will you need? Have you asked them for help yet?

Have you ever tried to catch a greased pig? Have you ever caught one? If you have, you've experienced a large success, but only if your name is Arnold M. Schopenhauer. What are the "greased pigs" you're chasing? Are they worth catching? What happens when you catch them? So what?

_____

_____

_____

_____

_____

_____

Exercise 4: What are the pictures that hold your attention the longest? Why? What are the mental pictures you find yourself observing most frequently—even without choosing to? These are the visualizations that are shaping the future you're unconsciously moving toward. Do you really want that kind of future for yourself and your loved ones—a future by default and not by design? How can you begin to design your future—starting today?

_____

_____

_____

_____

_____

_____

THE BASIS OF BEN'S BETTER SELF

Benjamin Franklin was one of the most successful early Americans. Which of his inventions is used most today? Bifocals, electricity, and the odometer are all used ubiquitously. His thirteen virtues perhaps *should* be used ubiquitously. Let's examine each of them individually.

Temperance: Eat not to dullness and drink not to elevation.

The Eighteenth Amendment to the United States Constitution, commonly referred to as "Prohibition," banned the manufacture, sale and transportation of intoxicating liquors. After nearly fourteen years it was repealed with the passage of the Twenty-first Amendment. Why? Because it was based in a false understand of temperance. Behind prohibition was the Temperance Movement. At first, pushing moderation, after several decades the focus of the Movement changed to complete prohibition of alcohol consumption.

This was not what Franklin had in mind. For him, individual choice was key. If you chose to consume alcoholic beverages, he would urge moderation so that they did not become "intoxicating liquors." This, too, was a choice for those who made the choice to drink.

Every choice leads to other choices and each choice arises from previous choices. The "chain of choice" you initiate each day is within your complete control.

The first choice of your day will determine how it winds up—fruitful or wasted. And what is that first choice you make? It usually is made on the subconscious level—how to approach the experiences you'll have. Will you approach them in a manic mode, perhaps a depressive one? Or will you deal with each as they occur in a temperate manner choosing to "moderate" the circumstances so that you gain—and maintain—a reasonable and rational view of what is actually going on in your life? If the latter, you'll find that you have a greater number of options from which to choose to make your experiences edifying and enriching for you and others.

As for food, he was advising moderate eating habits, especially avoiding gluttony, but if he lived today, he would probably have Americans eating a healthy diet—avoiding processed foods, including so-called "junk foods," so that we wouldn't become ill from our diets. What—and how—will YOU eat and drink today?

Silence: Speak not but what may benefit others or yourself. Avoid trifling conversation.

Have you ever been with somebody who talks too much? Have you ever met someone who engages in trifling conversation? Have you ever engaged in trifling conversation? If Franklin were transported to our times, he'd probably not like the pundits much. Would he like YOU?

I like the word game where you are asked to scramble the letters in a word to come up with as many other words as you can. Let's play that game. I'm going to make it easy on you. Instead of asking for as many words as you can come up with, I'm only going to ask you for a single word. Ready? OK. What other word can you see when you scramble the letters in the word, LISTEN?

Ready for the answer I'm looking for? It's SILENT. The two are interrelated, as it turns out, in more ways than one. You cannot listen when you are not silent.

A famous quote variously attributed to Abraham Lincoln and Mark Twain, but that probably originated with the English poet Samuel Johnson, says it best. The American version of the story is that a young newly elected Representative approached Abraham Lincoln and asked him if he should speak out during the debates on the floor. He thought that his colleagues might think him a fool if he didn't. Lincoln replied, "Better to remain silent and be thought a fool than to speak out and remove all doubt."

Order: Let all your things have their places. Let each part of your business have its time.

This is great advice for all of us—not just those engaged in business or commerce. From this wellspring flows the practice of time management. If you manage your time well—you will succeed, as time is the most crucial ingredient of everything you do. Be orderly and resolute in keeping order in your life and in your relationships. People will appreciate the structure. We all need appropriate boundaries within which we can channel our energies and efforts toward becoming our better Selves.

Timeliness is not a concept that is widely discussed. It means that there is a "right time" for things to happen. Each day will unfold only as each second passes—and not a moment faster. Each of your worthy aspirations will be fully manifested in its own time—and not a moment sooner. But you must be actively pursuing them before they can happen at all. You just need to be aware that, if you are pursuing them, they will happen in a *timely* manner.

Resolution: Resolve to perform what you ought. Perform without fail what you resolve.

Resolution is Ben's way of saying that, in order to accomplish anything of merit and worth, you must first be clear on what you want to accomplish. This is the foundation of commitment: knowing what you should be doing with your life and then making every effort to live in that manner.

Do not make any resolutions you are not really committed to making happen. Doing so will only make you feel bad about yourself when you fail to follow through.

Frugality: Make no expense but to do good to others or yourself. Waste nothing.

This is the principle of edification extended to the use of money. What did you spend your money on today? Did it, or will it, produce any real and lasting good for yourself and others? Do you feel you wasted anything today in terms of your time or your money? If so, resolve not to do it again.

Industry: Lose no time. Be always employed in something useful. Cut off all unnecessary actions.

Does this virtue apply only to people who are employed? Ben might say, "Most surely not. If you're unemployed, you should probably adhere to this principle with even greater tenacity." Lose no time seeking to wisely employ the talents and gifts you've been given. This is absolutely necessary to do. They exist to be used in the service of building up better Selves—yours and others'. Anything not moving you toward your better Self is unnecessary.

Sincerity: Use no hurtful deceit. Think innocently and justly; and, if you speak, speak accordingly.

Lies can ruin lives. This is why gossip is prohibited in the Bible and is frowned upon in most societies. It's time consuming, energy consuming, and a waste of both, not to mention stressful even for the most skilled of liars. Trying to keep up with your lies is like herding cats—just when you think you're making progress, they all eventually get "out of the bag."

Just as a physician's enterprise is known as a "practice," so, too, the enterprise of your life involves practices. In "practicing medicine," a doctor becomes better at diagnosing and treating disease and discomfort. In practicing your principles with sincerity, you're better able to manifest your worthy aspirations and become your better Self.

Justice: Wrong none by doing injuries or omitting the benefits that are your duty.

There are sins of commission and sins of omission—both can have destructive consequences. To know what would be helpful and beneficial to others and not do it is perhaps a greater sin than to inflict harm directly, although this is most certainly debatable. What do you think?

Justice is doing right by others under the law. Legally speaking, justice can be enforced. Anticipating one of my own principles to practice below, love is doing right by others regardless of the law. Such behavior can be neither legislated nor enforced. When Franklin speaks of "duty" he means empathic love that is born of a principled morality that goes beyond any system of laws.

Moderation: Avoid extremes. Forbear resenting injuries so much as you think they deserve.

Whenever you feel that you're living "on the edge" and are about to "fall off a cliff" keep in mind that you can choose to move away from danger, not just toward it. You can moderate your momentum toward your better Self.

Resenting injuries is another way of saying "holding a grudge." Think about holding a small glass of water out in front of you. Keep holding it and eventually that small glass of water, as simple a task as it started out being, becomes monumentally difficult. It's weight increases with each passing minute until it becomes unbearable. Yet we continue to hold on. By doing so, perhaps we think we're inflicting our own injury on the one who injured us. Ridiculous! You're only picking at the scab—and, as your mother told you, it will never heal.

Cleanliness: Tolerate no uncleanness in body, clothes, or habitation.

When you think well of yourself, you show it in the ways you treat yourself, your surroundings, your possessions and other people. If you fail to take care of your appearance and the place where you live is dirty and disheveled, what does this say about the picture you have of yourself? It's certainly not one of your *better Self*!

Perhaps Franklin isn't just referring to stinky people who live in dirty places. Could he also be advising you to help the genuine poor who, because of grinding poverty, do not see themselves as their better Selves and therefore worthy of cleanliness? If "cleanliness is next to godliness" and you feel abandoned by God, then why bother cleaning up?

Tranquility: Be not disturbed at trifles, nor at accidents common or unavoidable.

Some people get upset and experience an increase in their heart rate and blood pressure over things that don't matter. Richard Carlson's, *"Don't Sweat The Small Stuff . . . And It's All Small Stuff,"* says it all in the title of his book. What is some of the "small stuff" you're dealing with right now? Is it true that it's **all** small stuff? Think about what gets you all worked up. Is **that** small stuff?

Are you bothered by incidents that are accidents that could not have been avoided no matter how hard you tried? Let it go already!

What about common mistakes like mixing up your words saying, for instance, "He had to use a fire distinguisher" or "The monster is just a pigment of my imagination?" Have you ever embarrassed yourself by such confusion of terminology like, "Good punctuation means not to be late" or "He's a wolf in cheap clothing?" Come on, 'fess up. If not these exact mistakes, then something close to them—right? So what? Big deal. Let it go already! Be at peace and, as the Beatles used to sing, "let it be."

Chastity: Rarely use venery but for health or offspring; never to dullness, weakness, or the injury of your own or another's peace or reputation.

Self-discipline in the area of sexual expression is important for at least two reasons: 1) health and 2) sanity. Keep them both by making wise decisions that take both your better Self and the other's better Self into account. Poor choices in this area have led to countless life-long miseries for many.

The concept of sublimation is important here as it relates to self-discipline. Sublimation is channeling impulses into other creative, often less volatile and risky activities. It is the act of intentionally re-routing energy that arises from an essential human drive, like sex, to another area of action, like artistic expression or athleticism. Sublimation, by definition, demands self-discipline because it involves the act of choosing to acknowledge the original source of the energy and the willingness to use it for other purposes.

In other words, the energy associated with sexual drive doesn't necessarily have to be used for sexual expression. Human energies can be separated from their original sources and used to achieve ends unrelated to those sources. This is not to say, however, that sexual energy should be redirected to other outcomes in every instance. I am saying that you have a choice HOW to use your sexual energy to accomplish purposes not necessarily related to sex.

Is this a choice you really believe you have? If you do, then the act of choosing must come from a disciplined self—your better Self—or it will not be made at all.

Humility: Imitate Jesus and Socrates.

Who else would you add to this short list of those whom you should imitate—or perhaps are modeling yourself after at the moment? Who is the most humble person you know? Aside from humble, how else would you describe them? Would you like to be like them? If so, how can you? (Hint: you're reading about how you can right now).

Ken's Five More . . .

My five practices are a natural addendum to Franklin's thirteen axioms. Practice leads to mastery over whatever it is you're practicing. Practice these and you'll become the master of your better Self!

Patience

Practicing patience is time well spent—no matter how long it takes! People in a hurry may seem to get more done at the outset, but the effect is temporary at best. At worst, the effects are detrimental to goal achievement because often the work wasn't done right or well the first time and so must be done again.

This robs you of precious time and energy you need to get the right things done well so you can more quickly accomplish your goals. Do you like doing the same work over? When you had to perform rework, what were the causes for it? At the root of rework you'll normally find a lack of patience.

Patience is always rewarded. Honest and intelligent thought and effort are always rewarded. Do you believe this? Why or why not?

Persistence

Persistence is the sister of patience. Patience means little without persistence. Stick with it. Don't quit. Keep on keeping on. As the occasional sign on the street corner reads, "The end is near!" What end are *you* near? Are you near your better Self?

Kindness

We have all experienced kindness. When was the last time you were shown kindness? How did you feel? Were your motivated to demonstrate kindness to someone else that same day? How did *that* make you feel? What happened? How long did the effects last of both the kindness you experienced and the kindness you gave?

Practicing a selfless altruism without an ulterior motive is almost guaranteed to reveal not only YOUR better Self, but will often draw out the better Selves of those to whom you are showing kindness. Kindness, like a positive attitude, is contagious. Once loosed, it races throughout the community.

Positive Expectation

"This experience is going to be better than I ever could have imagined!" Yes, these words, when spoken immediately prior to anything you undertake, will set your mind on the straight and narrow path toward an outstanding, occasionally extraordinary experience. Don't believe it? Then you haven't tried it yet. What are you waiting for?

I heard this famous phrase for the first time only about a dozen years ago: **"If it is to be, it is up to me!"** I didn't believe it at first because it seemed too "cute." But believe me, nothing truer has ever been uttered. Expect to live as your better Self and, since it is up to you, you *will* discover creative and exciting ways to make it happen.

Love

The limits of love are those you set within your heart. In other words, if you choose not to set any, the love you show can be limitless. What this means is that love is a practice of NOT setting limits, or at least expanding the limits you have already placed within your heart or reducing their number.

This is not to say that the love you show should be undisciplined, arbitrary or undiscerning. Love is the practice of seeking to embrace the unlovable, the unloving, the shallow souls for whom love is a foreign notion—an alien emotion.

Practicing love is an exercise in walking the fine line between comfort and discomfort, confidence and hesitancy, faith and fear. But it is only by walking this line that you can truly know the power of the love that you are capable of showing by being your better Self.

Exercise 1: Have you read a biography of Ben Franklin? What do you think of him as a person? Was he perfect? Was he a perfect example of a human being who was using every bit of the resources of his better Self? Do you think Franklin was able to manifest every one of his worthy aspirations? Could you be like Ben? Would you want to?

_____

_____

_____

_____

_____

_____

Exercise 2: Which of Franklin's thirteen virtues most attracts your attention? Why? Do you think you should be working to improve in that specific area of your life? If so, how will you begin? What do you want to achieve? What kind of person, what kind of attributes, traits, characteristics and behaviors will you exhibit when you have improved in this single area? How will others talk about you "behind your back?"

_____

_____

_____

_____

_____

_____

Exercise 3: What time management techniques do you use regularly? Which ones actually work in helping you work both right and well? What is your definition of "timeliness?" Can you be successful without it? Why or why not?

_____

_____

_____

_____

_____

Exercise 4: Can you ever legislate morality? Can you ever force someone to treat others in a kind and respectful manner—or only punish them if they don't? Does virtue only arise from a disciplined mind and heart or can enforced behavior eventually result in a virtuous heart and benevolent mind?

_____

_____

_____

_____

_____

Exercise 5: The ancient Greeks emphasized moderation. What is moderation? What does moderation look like in your life? Why are excesses looked upon by the Greeks and Franklin, not to mention countless others, as detrimental to one's soul and success? How do you practice moderation today? Do your friends and family practice moderation? How can you help them if they don't? How can they help you if YOU don't?

List three benefits you are experiencing (or will experience) as you practice moderation in all things. What would cause you to be immoderate? Is there ever a good reason for immoderation?

_____
_____
_____
_____
_____
_____

Exercise 6: One a scale of 1 to 10 (10 = highest), how would you rate the level of tranquility in your life right now? If you're not happy with it, how will you increase it?

_____
_____
_____
_____
_____
_____

Exercise 7: Make sure you know what "venery" means. Do you know what "sublimation" means? If not, it will be difficult to understand what I'm saying here.

How do you deal with your sexual energy when it is inappropriate and/or unhealthy to express it? Can you think of any other ways you could sublimate that energy and channel it into other productive and equally satisfying endeavors?

_____
_____
_____
_____
_____

Exercise 8: What do you know about Jesus and Socrates? Why would you want to imitate either of them?

_____
_____
_____
_____
_____
_____

Exercise 9: How have you expressed humility in the past week? Why? What happened? How did you feel? Will you do it again? Under what circumstances?

_____
_____
_____
_____
_____
_____

Exercise 10: How much patience does it take to screw in a light bulb? How much patience does it take to hear the sound of one hand clapping? How much patience is required to fully understand another human being?

_____
_____
_____
_____
_____
_____

Exercise 11: Do you believe that honest intelligent thought and effort are always rewarded? If they are, what could the rewards be?

_____
_____
_____
_____
_____
_____

Exercise 12: What was the kindest thing anyone ever did for you? What was the kindest thing you ever did for someone else? Do you ever need a reason to show kindness?

_____

_____

_____

_____

_____

Exercise 13: What is up to you alone to make happen today?

_____

_____

_____

_____

_____

Exercise 14: When was the time you most needed someone to love you? Was someone there to love you? Who was it? How did they express their love for you? Did it help? What did you learn?

_____

_____

_____

_____

_____

Exercise 15: How have you loved another who was "unlovable?" What did you do? How did they react? Did it wind up helping? How do you know?

_____

_____

_____

_____

_____

Exercise 16: Is it difficult for you to express love? If so, why do you think so? What can you do to be more comfortable showing love for others?

_____

_____

_____

_____

_____

_____

THE POWER TO BE YOUR BETTER SELF

The habits you have developed over your lifetime form the basis of your personal power. These automatic actions comprise the foundation upon which your life is built. But the trouble with habits is that they're so habit-forming! Too often we become slaves to our habits, and end up going through the motions, settling for the mediocre because it's familiar, comfortable and predictable.

Habits can make us or break us. The power to be your better Self originates in your choice of whether you allow your habits to facilitate or hinder your movement toward your worthy aspirations. Habits are the results of successful practice. You can be a success at practicing a bad habit that will cause you to fail to achieve your worthy aspirations.

What are some of these "bad habits" you're practicing today? Keep in mind that such habits don't have to be described in terms of *actions*—they can also be described in terms of *INACTION*, meaning, you have habits of doing and habits of NOT doing, both, if bad, contribute to your eventual failure to achieve your goals. What are you in the habit of <u>not</u> doing right now that, if you did, would help you more easily and quickly manifest your worthy aspirations?

_____
_____
_____
_____
_____
_____

Exercise 1: How will what you're practicing today become helpful habits that will move you closer to where you want to be and what you want to have in your life? Think about how your "habitual self" is sabotaging your better Self. What are you going to do about that?

_____
_____
_____
_____
_____

Exercise 2: Do you yearn to do better than what you've been doing—including doing better than what you think your "best" is—in life and work? Why aren't you doing any better now?

_____

_____

_____

_____

_____

_____

What is getting in your way? I will hazard a guess on your behalf: you haven't yet made a firm decision to use your habits to create excellence and extraordinary results in your life. When you decide to do so, you will take off like a bullet moving toward the reality of your better Self. How will you make the choice—today—to strive for excellence so you can exceed your "best?"

_____

_____

_____

_____

_____

How can you begin to stop what's stopping you?

_____

_____

_____

_____

_____

YOUR CHILD IS WAITING

Your better Self is childlike in nature. This means that you look at the world and your specific circumstances and situations as promises for a better future rather than the culmination of a distasteful past. You can see the world in this way when you look at your life as possessing an embryonic potential that everyday presents itself anew.

Children wake up every day filled with the giddy sense of newness and renewal. This inward outlook drives creative activity toward the manifestation of their worthy aspirations. They can barely wait to experience again their better Selves in everything they do.

What does it mean to be childlike as an adult?

There was much laughter—so much so that cheeks and sides and stomachs were beginning to hurt. The setting was the afterglow of a fine dinner as we relaxed in comfortable seating: overstuffed chairs hosting overstuffed guests.

The conversation gravitated to occasions when our dress was . . . how shall I say . . . unfashionable. We laughed at a time when one of us had gone through an important social engagement wearing different kinds—and colors—of shoes. Another related a similar situation except that it was different kinds of earrings she was wearing throughout the event. Still other stories of "faux pas" brought more laughter—and comfort knowing that we were not the only ones to have experienced such embarrassments.

When the evening came to a close, I felt refreshed, invigorated and "exercised." I felt like a kid again.

Who were these people whose energetic playfulness and joy of living reintroduced me to my inner child? Four ladies in their eighties and nineties!

Remember how you were as a small child—innocent, eager, filled with anticipation and wonder? Life was fresh and everything was possible. Living as your better Self, it can be that way again—at any age.

> **Exercise:** Think about the elderly people in your life. List five characteristics they have that you admire. Would you like to be like them when you're their age? Would you like to be like them right now? Have any of these people helped you recapture the childlike nature of your better Self? Could they? Is age important when it comes to being your better Self? Why do you say that?

The Biggest Mistake You Can Make

Children are not afraid to make mistakes. Do you think that's true? If it is true, when do they begin to learn to be afraid of making mistakes? When did YOU? Are you still afraid?

As older children, and later as adults, fear can paralyze us. The greatest mistake you can make is to let fear overwhelm your desire to become your better Self, halting your onward march toward achieving your worthy aspirations.

Mistakes occur as a result of a lack of diligence in adhering to your personal set of boundaries and values. Mistakes, however, are opportunities to being again more intelligently to manifest your worthy aspirations because now you know what doesn't work or what you don't want to happen again.

Exercise 1: What is the biggest mistake you ever made? In what ways did you not adhere to your personal set of boundaries and values that resulted in this mistake being made? What were its consequences? Are you still dealing with them today? What have you learned from this mistake? Have you made this mistake more than once? If you have, what can you do today that will help you learn from it more than you have already—so you don't make it yet again?

_____
_____
_____
_____
_____
_____

Exercise 2: How do you learn from your mistakes? Do you have a plan to learn from them? Consider the following to help you structure such a plan:

1) Intentionally seek situations where you can make "interesting" mistakes. What is an "interesting" mistake? It's one whose consequences are actually better than anything you could have planned for; in other words, your plan to learn from your mistakes should include preparing to be pleasantly surprised. Sometimes mistakes turn out to be blessings in disguise.

2) Admit your mistakes—first to yourself, then to those impacted by their "fallout" and finally to your "diary" (write a brief story about what you did or didn't do, why you think you did it or didn't do it, the consequences of what you did or didn't do, what you have learned from it and your plan to begin again more intelligently).

3) Make changes in your habits that result in better outcomes—those that move you closer and faster to manifesting your worthy aspirations. How? Listen to the inner voice of your better Self—you'll hear everything you need to know to make the right changes in your life—starting today.

_____

_____

_____

_____

_____

_____

Exercise 3: What has your inner voice been telling you lately? Can't hear it? Do you want to hear it? If so, just listen right now to nothing in particular. Silently ask yourself, "What do I hear my better Self saying to me?" Write down your first impressions. What do you think they mean? Are they realistic to achieve? What would happen if you took action on what you heard today?

_____

_____

_____

_____

_____

_____

Mistakes will happen, of course. But your better Self can make mistakes better . . . and make "better" mistakes!

EPILOGUE

When it comes to manifesting your worthy aspirations and becoming your better Self, instant gratification often results in long-term dissatisfaction and despair. You may feel great at the moment of getting what you think you want at the time—but the ramifications for achieving your goals are very often not good.

If you prepare to realize your goals by practicing your principles within beneficial boundaries, you WILL summon the power, passion and purpose of your better Self. Like Sam Clemens said once, you can and will leave the comfortable shores of your current state to explore, dream and discover your better Self. Even if it takes longer than a few weeks, months or even years, when it occurs, you know without a doubt the full experience of gratification.

> **Exercise:** Did you seek instant gratification today? What did you do? Why? What would happen if you had delayed your gratification until, say, tomorrow, or even until next week or next month? Could your enjoyment have been greater later? Could you have accomplished more than what you did if you had delayed your gratification? What do you need to "put on hold" right now that would prove to be much more gratifying and beneficial to do sometime in the future?

_____

_____

_____

_____

_____

_____

Your better Self is an explorer at heart. It sets out in search of new ways to express itself in its mission to help others become their better Selves. It explores new shores, different seas, strange lands. What new realms of your life and of the world are you exploring today?

POSTSCRIPT

Kahlil Gibran wrote, "The reality of the other person lies not in what he reveals to you but in what he cannot reveal to you. Therefore, if you would understand him, listen not to what he says but rather to what he does not say." This is especially true when you listen to the voice of your own better Self. Your better Self will speak through your thoughts, words and feelings to help you pursue and realize your worthy aspirations.

"The more faithfully you listen to the voice within you," wrote the Swedish General Secretary of the United Nations in the 1950's, Dag Hammarskjold, "the better you hear what is sounding outside. And only he who listens can speak." Speak the truth of your better Self only after you have listened for its voice proclaiming its presence in everything you do.

> **Exercise:** Become still and listen for the voice of your better Self. What is it saying? Can't hear it? Listen longer. Listen with your heart—that is, don't assign any mental meaning to any sensation or stimuli you experience. Contemplate their meaning later. Within your stillness the still, small voice speaks—at first faintly, gradually growing to a shout—proclaiming, "You have everything you need! Let your better Self lead! Let your better Self be!"

_____

_____

_____

_____

_____

_____

As I closed out the book with a poem, one of my own, *"See Into Forever,"* I'd like to end this companion self-study manual with a poem by "Anonymous," entitled, *"Today I Smiled."* Let your better Self smile today—and every day—because you are peaceful in your presence and powerful in your purpose to manifest every one of your worthy aspirations before you leave this world.

Today I smiled, and all at once,
Things didn't look so bad.
Today I shared with someone else,
A bit of hope I had.
Today I sang a little song,
And felt my heart grow light.
And, walked a happy little mile,
With not a cloud in sight.

Ken Wallace

Today I worked with what I had,
And, longed for nothing more;
And what had seemed like only weeds,
Were flowers at my door.
Today I loved a little more,
Complained a little less;
And, in the giving of myself,
Forgot my weariness.

OBSERVATIONS AND INSIGHTS

Some Tools to Help You Become Your Better Self

The following two pages contain worksheets that will help you clarify your worthy aspirations, identify the goals you need to set to help you manifest them in your everyday reality, and provide you with a better understanding of what you're dealing with in your current situation. They will also assist you to create specific ways to overcome any obstacles you're facing and to capitalize on opportunities that might be staring you in the face. Lastly, these worksheets can reveal creative methods to practically apply what you learn about yourself that will benefit others in your personal and professional life.

Using the "I Am Going to 'B'" worksheet, in the "Where Am I Now?" box at the bottom, identify a specific problem or opportunity you're being confronted with; be as detailed as you can in describing your current situation out of which this problem/opportunity arises. Next, visualize the new and improved situation in the cloud at the top of the sheet. This is where you want to be ("B"). Finally, record the specific steps you will take that will take you to your new, better reality. If you need more room, use the back of the sheet. Don't limit yourself to the three steps in the "What I Will Do to Get to 'B'" box at the upper left corner.

The "T2" ("Thought Time") worksheet is self-explanatory. Write the topic of your thinking time at the top of the page. Spend at least ten minutes "just thinking" about this topic. Use this tool to tap the strength and creativity of the inner resources of your better Self that will help you manifest your worthy aspirations and achieve your personal and professional goals regarding this particular area of your life.

Don't forget that other people in your life affect whether or not you will be successful. Be specific about what you need from them to succeed as well as how they will be positively affected by the changes you're going to make in the ways you conduct your life. Be playful and imaginative; try "thinking outside the box" refusing to filter your thoughts or to only "color within the lines." What you'll discover is that you not only have what it takes to become your better Self, but that you can take what you have and actually become your better Self . . . today.

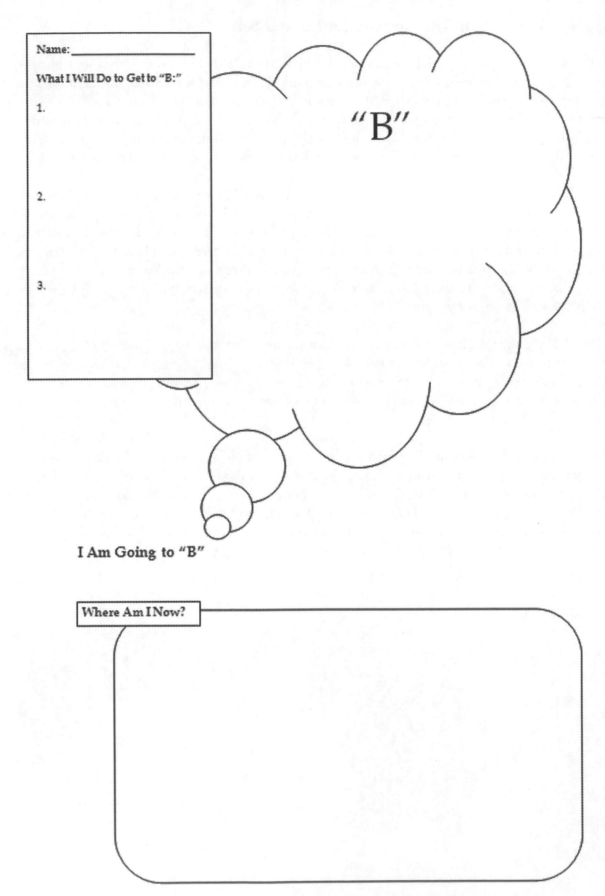

Name: _____

What I Will Do to Get to "B:"

1.

2.

3.

"B"

I Am Going to "B"

Where Am I Now?

Think Time (T2) Capture Sheet

Name:_____Date:_____T2 Topic: _____

Images/feelings/thoughts that occur to me regarding this topic (don't filter, just write):

_____
_____

Insights about these (what could these images/feelings/thoughts mean?):

_____
_____

Ideas that occur to me (how do these insights apply to the current situation?):

_____
_____

What are the possible benefits of this idea (these ideas) for . . .
Our company?

_____
_____

Our community?

_____
_____

Myself?

_____
_____

My family?

_____
_____

Playground (be a kid and draw, doodle, cut, paste . . . be your playful, creative Self):

_____
_____